SOCIAL MEDIA MARKETING 2020

Strategies to Become an Influencer with Facebook,
Instagram, Youtube and Twitter, Grow Your
Personal Brand Fast in 2020 and Beyond

RONALD GARY

TABLE OF CONTENTS

INTRODUCTION

The following chapters will discuss social media marketing—and even better, how you can use it to propel your business forward into money-making galore. Sounds great, right? It is.

In the world that we live in, people really underestimate social media. This is a giant mistake. Social media has completely changed our lives and how we live them. Business owners, especially, can't ignore it, as more and more people flock to the platforms to look for information on their favorite brands.

The reality is that your social media presence *does* affect how your business is perceived. People just expect you to have some sort of online account—and if you don't, it could negatively impact your business. You really don't want that, do you?

You're probably finding a lot of this overwhelming. Maybe this is why you picked up this book. However, never mind—you'll find that this will help you out. From figuring out which platform to use to a guide to each of the four major social networking websites online, this book has it all! You'll walk away from reading this book feeling as if you can do anything—well, at least, in terms of social media marketing.

CHAPTER 1: WHY SOCIAL MEDIA MARKETING IN 2020

Social media marketing can come off as incredibly complicated. There's picking out which one you want to use on your platform; there's choosing a niche and a topic you wish to talk about; there are followers and subscribers and everything else under the sun you can think of. All of this is confusing, so it's no wonder that a lot of businesses just choose not to bother at all. Instead, they go for the route of just pretending that social media doesn't exist and blindly go for the same old advertising and marketing methods that worked for them in the past.

Don't be that person.

No, instead, be the person who embraces change and fully accepts that we're living in a new era. There's no room for a business that doesn't participate in social media marketing on some level or another. Social media's impact is huge, and nobody can deny that. Not only that, but it's growing and growing every day, with more and more people creating accounts online. The number of people who use social media and the internet will only keep growing until everyone on the planet has an account of some kind.

If you're still not sold on the idea, check out these statistics:

- 3.2 billion people, about 42% of the global population, use some form of social media.
- Facebook is the most widely used platform. 68% of adult Americans say that they are Facebook users.

- 90% of millennials, 77% of generation X, and 48% of baby boomers use social media regularly. These numbers will likely go even higher up with the generation X as they reach adulthood and are able to join a lot of these platforms.
- The average person spends about 2 hours and 22 minutes on social media every day.
- 73% of business owners who use social media marketing say that they think that participating in social media has been "very good" for business.
- 54% of social media users say that they have used, or currently use, social media to investigate a product that they're considering purchasing. 1 in 3 people has made a purchase through social media. This is the stat that should really get you onto a social media platform.
- 91% of social media users access their favorite social media platforms on mobile devices. This shouldn't come as a surprise to anyone, considering that we carry our phones everywhere. However, it's still a useful thing to know, as you can build your content around the idea that someone will be consuming it on a mobile device.

Now, after reading all of these stats, are you sure you don't want to be on social media? Yeah, I bet you do. It's not hard, reading these stats above, to realize that you may just need social media marketing for your business. That's just facts.

Here are just a couple more of the amazing benefits that social media marketing has:

1. **More brand awareness.** On social media, there is a whole group of people who have never heard of you, and social media is one of the easiest, cheapest ways to reach them. You can engage with a broad audience of consumers, and bringing them closer to your brand. 91% of marketers have reported that their social media efforts made more people aware of their business.

2. **You're easier to find.** While there aren't many businesses out there that don't have a website of some kind, being able to find you on social media will bring more people to your website. Think of it almost like you're just adding more doorways to your house, making it easier for people to find the entrance and actually get in. Not only that, but different people search in different ways. Hence, by having a social media account, they may be able to find you easier by using keywords. Eventually, after a certain amount of time, you'll rank higher in a lot of search engine's algorithms, appearing higher up on the page. The longer you're on social media, the more chance you have on getting onto that first page of Google. Because let's face it, who exactly goes past the first page?

3. **More trust between you and your customers.** With social media marketing, you can easily bring out the

more humane side of your brand that traditional advertising doesn't allow for. You can really give a positive vibe with a few posts, giving your brand a personality. One of the rules of selling is remembering that people are more likely to buy from people than brands, and social media is not the place to forget that rule. With social media, you can build trust with your customers, both current and future. This will lead to them more likely to think of you when they need your services.

4. **Better customer satisfaction.** As if the fact that you're now building trust with your customers isn't enough, now, you actually satisfy them more. Having customers is almost like having a significant other. Just like with a spouse, you have to communicate with your customers, listening to their needs and responding to them. This leads to higher satisfaction for them, as they feel like they're being heard. Remember, social media was built for the sole reason of staying in touch with people. Hence, remember to stay in touch with your customer base. This means being attentive, replying to their comments and messages, and addressing concerns as soon as you get them. Every interaction on your account is another opportunity to publicly prove to the world that your customer service is the best of the best. This will be seen in a positive light, from both the customer that you interacted with to any potential customers skimming your timeline. Customers want to be able to

reach their favorite brands easily, and social media is the perfect place to do so.

5. **Loyalty from customers.** It's said that once you develop a solidly loyal base, you're set for life. Loyalty in a customer base is a valuable thing, and anything that can be done to strengthen that loyalty should be done. Customer satisfaction and brand loyalty go together like peanut butter and jelly. This means that if communicating with your audience on social media helps with customer satisfaction, it will help with brand loyalty as well. Not only that, but the millennial generation is also known for being incredibly loyal to their favorite brands, with 62% of them more loyal with brands that communicate with them. Considering that right now these are the people who are on the internet the most in the current climate, that's an important thing to consider.

6. **Controlling the conversation**. With a social media account, you can control the conversation surrounding your brand much more easily than if you don't have a social media account. You decide what goes out there when. Not only that but having a social media account comes off as more credible than those businesses that don't have one. This means that you're not only controlling the conversation, but you're also participating in the larger one happening online, whether it's about your niche or something else.

7. **It's not a big investment, money wise**. When you consider just how much money different brands

spend on your basic, everyday advertising that you see on TV or on billboards, it's hard not to flinch or recoil in some way. In contrast, social media is the freest form of advertising you will ever get. It's completely free to sign up for, and any advertising you choose to do on the platform is entirely up to you. Not only that, but it's surprisingly cheap. Not only that but on social media, people will do the advertising for you. They'll do this by talking about you, sharing your posts, and more. Free Ads? Who wouldn't want that?

8. **You're getting information directly from your customers**. In the days of your run of the mill advertising, businesses had to rely on poll numbers. While usually accurate, in some cases they were not, which could mean that the business had spent money on ads that didn't work. When it's social media, you hear right from the consumers—word for word. Head into the comment section of any major business page, and you'll find dozens, if not hundreds, of suggestions and requests from consumers. You can see your customer's interests and needs by directly talking to them. Not having a social media account means that you're missing out on this great information. Not only that, but social media analytical tools will help you figure out exactly what the demographics of your audience is (you should already know this when you go into it, but the analytics might inform you of something you didn't know before).

9. **Establishing your expertise**. If people are consistently finding valuable information on your page, you're showing that you're actually knowing what you're talking about. This is an easy way to establish your expertise in the field. Think of it this way: would you prefer to have a doctor that has just his degrees on his walls, or would you prefer to have a doctor with his degrees on his walls, but also medical journals and magazines spread around? If you post a lot not just about your business, but also just about your industry in general, it proves to your fans that you're keeping up with the latest of what's going in. You're paying attention.

Cons

Of course, as with everything, there are cons to social media. There aren't too many things with some sort of part of it that just isn't so great. While there are a lot of huge benefits to social media and it is totally worth it to take part in it, it doesn't hurt to know the struggles going in. Here, we've listed both the issues that you may face, plus instructions on how to deal with them.

1. **Trolls**. Once you have been on social media for a certain amount of time, you'll become aware of what are known as "trolls." Basically, these are people who go into parts of the internet and write comments specifically to get people riled up. Basically, they want the reaction, and they find it hilarious. Trolls can be annoying, but they're just part of life when it

comes to the internet. They want to argue; they want to make people angry. Hence, the key is here not to give them that reaction. Don't respond to them. Report the comment, especially if it's threatening in nature, and get it removed. Don't give them any of your time, and don't reply to their comments. There is one exception to that rule, however. And that's basically this: only if you can really take them on, wit for wit, and pulverize their argument to pieces with something funny. This is how many brands, and people, have been dealing with trolls online, by simply turning their argument on them in a funny way. This is likely to get a lot of attention and love on whatever platform you're using. Just be sure that it's actually witty.

2. **Negative feedback**. Now, this isn't necessarily trolls online. This is just unsatisfied customers. These can be dangerous for your business, as other people can check out your social media and see the comments. This may lead to them not wanting to give you any business altogether. This is the last thing that you want. Yes, you may have 99 glowing positive reviews, but that 1 bad review can really tear you down, as that will be the one that people remember. The solution to this is really quite simple: don't just let it die. Address it. Reach out to them. Talk through exactly why they're unhappy and what you can do to fix whatever issue they're having. The situation could be one that is easily fixed, and they may just

take back their bad review and rectify the matter. Basically, just act as if you would in a store where a customer brought back a defect product.

3. **It can eat up time**. While yes, social media is free in terms of dollars, it is not free when it comes to time. After all, time is money, right? Not only that, but there is a learning curve, and there is a huge amount of underestimation when it comes to the amount of hard work that goes into a successful social media marketing campaign. Especially if you're working by yourself without a team to help you out, you have to keep your profiles updated and polished, consistently post updates, and provide valuable information on whatever it is you're all about, which can take hours of effort. Not only that but oftentimes it takes months or even years of grinding on social media before marketers even see a difference. All of this means that people often give up before they even begin, often because they feel overwhelmed and like they don't know what they're doing. There are solutions to this. One thing you can do is someone else do all the work for you. These people are called Social Media Marketers, but they can very expensive and run up a large tab very quickly. If you can't afford it, don't. Maybe have a few sessions with one, if it's your budget, who will help you come up with a strategy and a brilliant strategy out of the gate. What you really should be doing is focusing on only one at a time—to only master one social media platform at once. Just educating yourself as much as possible,

and considering that you bought this book, you're already halfway there. Knowing your chosen platform inside and out will really help you navigate it easier, and you will probably see success a lot earlier thanks to that. Just one page will really increase your revenue, and while there are plenty of people out there who want to have as many pages as possible, this just isn't very effective in the long run. This means that you should completely master one social media platform before you go to another one. Just one at a time. When you know the entire platform backward and forward, then you can move onto another one. The most important thing to remember is that yes, it's time-consuming, but it will be worth it in the end. Besides, a year from now you'll be thinking to yourself "I should've started" anyway.

4. Something you say is taken out of context. One thing that a lot of brand's social media pages have run into is saying something, meaning it one way, then their followers and the members of the internet taking it in an entirely different way. Spell check issues have been another thing that's plagued business accounts. This kind of thing can really be disastrous for your business, especially if the meaning is making light of something serious (like a current news event). The solution to this is really simple; CHECK. Spell check everything. Get someone else to read it over (especially long posts, where things are easier to miss). Keep up with current news so that you make sure you're not accidentally referring to issues. If you're

using hashtags, make sure to look to see what other people are saying before you jump onto the band-wagon. This means that every post needs to be thought out.

Now, in this chapter, we basically covered everything to do with why you should be on social media, plus being honest about the fact that yes, there are downsides (that can be remedied easily). Now, we're going to get really into social media and you. Figuring out where you should be, what kind of brand you are, and carving out your own little spot on the internet.

CHAPTER 2: WHERE TO SPEND TIME

One of the biggest mistakes a lot of business people make in terms of social media marketing is that they forget that the internet is really just a community of people. And in each community, there are always groups of some kind. When you go on the internet, you want to make sure that you're joining the community where people will look for you and want to listen to you.

This means that you need to figure out the social media platform that your audience is spending time on. Not only that, but you need to know everything about what image you want to put forward to really figure out exactly what you're going for. What kind of message do you want to come with your brand? Instantly figuring this out will help you decide where you want to be.

In this chapter, we're going to cover some simple dos and don'ts, figuring out your niche, and taking a look at each social media network and why you should be on it. Plus, we have a whole section on the different types of tools you should have for basic social media networking that will help charge your posts up with value. All of this information will not only help you find your people on the site but how to impress them in the best way possible.

First, let's go over some simple dos and don'ts that you should be following, no matter what social media platform that you're on. When you come up with a strategy for your social marketing, these tips will really help you figure out what you're supposed to be doing. Not only that, but they'll keep you on track of exactly where you were going. Read on.

- Do repurpose content. This means that reposting articles, sharing photos, other things. It will save you time and energy. Not only that, but you can share the same content to multiple different forms of social media.

- Don't do it in a cheap way. This means doing it over and over again. Be thoughtful about it, and change some elements in the post if you can. Maybe the last time you shared the article, it was a current thing. Maybe this time when you share it, do it in a throwback way so people can understand something else. Not only that but if you share it to multiple forms of social media, make sure to tweak it slightly so that it fits in with the network. What works on Facebook won't work on Instagram all the time and vice versa.

- Do Engage. This can be a difficult one for people to master on social media, as it's something that is a bit tricky. Getting people to like, comment, share, or follow you on social media requires a lot of work, especially since the higher engagement rate you have, the more people you're getting exposed to. One simple way that marketers invoke responses in their audience is to ask questions of their audience.

- Don't ignore your customers. What's the point of having a social media account unless you actually want to talk with your customers? Not paying attention to the people posting on your page is one of the easiest ways that your marketing strategy will fail. People don't want to follow and buy from brands who don't care about people's opinion. Not only that, but there may be some pretty amazing ideas in your comment section, you just have to look for them.

- Do keep calm in a crisis. If you're having issues with trolls or negative comments, or even if you just started some sort of issue, breath. Stay calm. It's not the end of the world. There are plenty of businesses out there who have done very stupid things online, and they turn out fine. Just be sure to address it immediately and come up with a strategy on how to deal.

- Don't just let anyone run your account. If you do plan on having someone run your account, make sure that they understand the message and tone you're trying to put across. Don't just let someone go crazy with your account. Make sure they know what they should be doing.

- Do pay attention. By pay attention, I mean that pay attention to what's going on in your chosen niche, and what's going on social media at the moment. That pertains to checking out the hashtag page, looking at memes, and knowing what people are talking about on the platform right now. Participating in the community will reflect well on you, and show that you're paying attention. Plus, you can show that you have a bit of a sense of humor, and it definitely will humanize you.

- Don't use bots. There are plenty of accounts out there who are using bots to help them grow, whether it's through liking or replying to comments. This is a mistake, as people can really tell when it's just an automated bot on the other side of the screen. Create content that's personal and thoughtful. Let yourself shine through. You can't do this with a bot. Not only that, but bots aren't actually allowed on social media networks. If you're caught, you'll be shut down and lose everything.

- Do understand that you can't be on every social media network. I know, I know, you just googled "social media networks" and found about 25 of them that you're not on. Now all you want to do is create a whole bunch of ghost towns on social media, accounts that you don't use that you don't have time for. This will reflect badly on your brand. Remember, one at a time, and don't go higher than maybe 5. Keeping up with 5 accounts will take up a lot of time just by themselves, even if you are reusing content and that's enough.

- Don't forget the current followers. It's easy to become obsessed with just gaining more followers without addressing the ones that you have. Remember, people follow you for a reason, so you need to pay attention to them. Just like you would nurture a relationship with a customer over a long time, you need to do the same with your followers. Don't forget them. After all, you don't want them to unfollow you!

These are just some basic dos and don'ts. Following these will really help smooth out your strategy and keep yourself on track. Now, let's talk about your niche and how to find it.

Quality Over Quantity

This age-old saying that no doubt somebody has said to you at some point or another works best when it comes to art. Whether or not you believe social media marketing is an art form, it definitely requires a lot of attention and finesse. This means that there should be no post that you put out that doesn't get attention. Every post is important. None of them should be given less attention than others. Each one will reflect your brand and your company, and you want the quality to be at the center of this whole thing. Believe it or not, but how your social media page is groomed and kept will reflect your whole brand. Your entire company. So keep it updated, well maintained, and make sure that every post is going out as perfect as it can be.

Consistency Is Key

To really succeed on social media, keeping things consistent on your page will help your business tremendously. This means consistent with everything; when you post, how you post, what your messaging is on your profile, everything. Everything needs to line up perfectly. This may sound like a big deal, but it's really not. It just requires effort and upkeep. You constantly have to ask yourself; does this post reflect what I want my business to stand for? Does this match up with the niche and tone of my profile? Just keep asking your-self these questions, and you'll do fine. It may take some practice to really nail consistency, so don't be too hard on yourself, at least at first.

Tools You May Need

To truly ace at social media marketing, you're really going to have to have a set of tools. Social media is just another craft in itself, and what do you need to make the best crafts? You need tools. Not everything on this list is completely mandatory, but it sure does help. These will not only help keep your posts in high quality and engaging for your audi-ences but will also help you reach your goals. Remember, quality over quantity, always. Consistency is important. These tools will also help you with these things as well.

A Computer and Smartphone: this is a no brainer. You're going to need a good computer and a smartphone to make use of all of the features on each platform, and you're going to need a smartphone if you want to be continually checking up on them and updating them throughout the day. That's just common sense.

Calendar: by a calendar, I mean a posting calendar. A calendar you keep to keep track of all of the posts you plan on doing, and when you plan on putting them onto your feed. Whether they're photos, videos, or text posts—you name it—these should be going up onto your calendar. You should be staying ahead of schedule, making sure that you're starting to plan Christmas posts in October or even earlier. These weeks passed quickly, and having a set plan in place will really help you stay on track.

A Good Camera Setup: You're probably, at some point or another, going to start making visual media, such as pictures and videos. This means that you'll probably likely have to invest in a good camera. What you choose to use for your camera really depends all on you, and what your needs for. While you could definitely get the best of the best, it just may not be practical for you. The newest and best cameras can easily run into $5,000, easily. That's not even counting in things like lighting, lenses, and other setups like sound. This kind of thing will really depend on your channel, but you can get a basic camcorder that will serve you well for under $500. It will have all the basic functions you need and is a good starting point when all you want is something to make good videos with. In fact, you could even just use your phone if you want just not to spend any money at all. Smartphone cameras have become increasingly better and better every year, and it's only a matter of time before they become so good that you can barely notice the difference between them and that of a high-resolution camera. We're going to be going over a bit in our YouTube channel on how to set up your videos and tips on making them really good, so that information is coming for you. But if you do plan on making videos or posting photos, you are going to need a camera at least, if not more.

Photo Editor: yes, you're going to need a photo editing system. Your first thought might be Photoshop, but you don't quite need something as complicated as that. In fact, you could literally do this right from your phone if you really wanted to. Of course, Photoshop isn't a bad idea if you can afford it or if you know how to use it, but if you don't, don't bother. There's a pretty steep learning curve, and if you just don't feel like you have the time to master it, it's definitely not necessary. Instead, check out these options for photo editors with all of the basic features that you will need:

Snapseed: this easy-to-use Google-made app is free to use. It has a lot of filters to choose from, and you can even use ones you personalize. You can insert text over photos, play with things like the exposure and contrast, and even save filters that you like so you can use them over and over again. It may be a little tricky to navigate, but for the most part, it's easy to get on board.

VSCO: This is the app that you hear about when social media marketers talk about photo editing apps. It's available through both the Apple App Store and Google Play Store and has all of the features you come to expect from a photo editing app. It's the great filters that make the app really shine. Even in the free version, it has a great variety of them, and will actually help you select which ones work best for your photo. Not only that, but it's easy to navigate, so you'll figure everything out right off the bat.

Photoshop: I know, I know, I just said that having a really fancy photo editor isn't necessary. And it's not. However, if you're willing to take the time to learn how to use it and you don't mind paying for it, there isn't much you can't do with Photoshop. Of course, only get this one if you feel like you really need it. If you just want to do some basic photo editing, stick to one of these apps.

Video Editor: Similar to photo editing, people's first inclination is to buy the fanciest editor they can get their hands on, something like Apple's FinalCut Pro or Adobe's Premiere Pro. However, also just like photo editing, there are plenty of options out there that don't involve so much time invested in mastering them. Admittedly, unlike with photo editors, there are a lot less really good video editing apps out there. However, there are options that can be used on your computer no problem that does a lot of the stuff you likely plan to do anyway.

iMovie: this is only available through Apple, but is a great little video editor. Perfect for beginners, it's easy to use and has a lot of basic functions that you'll find in pretty much every major video app. You can add title cards, audio, and more.

Windows Movie Maker: this is probably the thing that you used when you were editing a video for school as a teenager. It's a staple on every windows computer, and it's easy to use.

There aren't a lot of functions on here that are super advanced, and it pretty much only has the most basic of tools. But it's good if you just want something super simple.

InShot: this useful little app is available on both Android and iOS, and it's perfect if you just want to make little clips right from your phone or tablet. It lets you do all of the basic things you need from an editing app, and the full version is not too expensive. Things such as cutting, splitting, and adding text can all be done from this app and right from your phone.

FinalCut Pro/Premiere Pro: Just like with Photoshop, it doesn't hurt knowing how to use these. Especially since you can do a lot of other things with these platforms as opposed to the others listed here, such as adding different texts, color correcting, and more. There is a learning curve, of course, and FinalCut Pro is only available through Apple, but it may be worth it to learn. Video editing is a pretty useful skill to have.

Figuring Out Your Social Media Niche

Figuring out your niche should be pretty simple for this. After all, your niche is probably all figured out. You already know what you're selling, or at least what you want to sell. Whether you're selling an online course or a child's toy, you should already have an idea of what kind of message you want to send out there. Figuring out your social media niche is a bit of a different subject. You already know what you're selling—now, you just have to figure out where you can go to find them.

The first step is that you need to understand your audience. How old are they? What do they like? What do they respond to? Where do they live? What's their gender? Are they married or single? Do they have children? What kind of foods do they like? What do their day to day lives look like? How much money do they make?

You don't have to answer every question here, and there are some questions that aren't even on that list. What questions you ask yourself to identify your audience are up to you, but in general, it's usually based on age, gender, and class.

Asking yourself these questions will help you figure out exactly where they're spending on their time online. Different people have different preferences in where they spend their time online, just as they do in the real world. Your job is to figure out exactly where these people are.

Figuring out your audience can be a bit difficult. If you already have some form of social media, checking out your analytics (if it has it) will probably help. Another way is just to figure out who you're selling to. You may not always be right, but it's a good start.

The next thing you need to do is understand your goals. What do you want to accomplish on social media? Are you plan ning on spending money? How much? What is the end goal for this campaign? Having a clear goal will also help you pick out a social media market that fits you the best. Here are a few suggestions:

- Increasing awareness
- Giving personality
- Connecting with customers
- Showing leadership
- Improving your reputation
- Getting people interested and talking

While all of these are great goals, avoid doing more than one or two of them at once. Having a narrow mindset with what you want out of social media, at least at first, will really help you aim your focus in a productive way. This will lead to you getting more out of it. Picking your social media goals will largely help you with picking out which social media you eventually choose.

Understand each of their options. We cover 4 social media networks in this book, all of them the big kids on the block. But there is a huge pile of social media networks out there, and picking just one will really help narrow it down. It's important to know each purpose they have and how they work—not even a thorough understanding of them, just a general idea. This can help make your decision a lot easier.

We've included a quick guide to each of the networks in this book, so once you have read through them, now it's time to pick and rank them. Base this ranking on what you need, who your audience is, what they want, and how the platform will align with the content that you have in mind.

Follow this quick guide for ranking:

1. Check out your competitors. Looking at your competitors can help you choose which network you should be on. If there is a business that's similar to

yours, check out what they're doing. You may get some ideas on what kind of content you want to put out and how you choose to carry yourself on social media.

2. Ask yourself how active do you want to be. Do you want to post one to three times a day? Eight times a day? Once a day? Once a week? Every two weeks? Think of your schedule and how you'll make this work.

3. What type of content do you want to post? Do you plan on making a lot of short and sweet text posts? Do you plan on responding directly to your followers through the account? Are you going to be posting a lot of pictures and videos? How much production do you want to put into them?

Then, it's time to pick. Take a look now at our guides to each social media network, and ask yourself the above questions as you look. The purpose of these guidelines is to do a quick skim over the four networks covered in this book, and point out what kind of business should be on them. Then, once you've chosen your network, then you can head to its chapter for its guide to how to make the most of the platform.

Facebook

Facebook brags of 1.5 billion active users, 3 billion overall. These numbers alone make it the one social media platform that is nearly impossible to ignore. However, the fact that it's a hard one to master has a lot of people turning away from it.

Using Facebook to its full potential is tricky. You really need to insert personality, personalization, and regular reader interaction. It's a great network to be on, and with that many users, it's hard to avoid. It really requires a lot of attention when it comes to replying to comments and posts.

Here are some demographics to give you a better idea of who's on the platform:

Gender
Men: 66%
Women: 77%

Age
18 to 29: 87%
30 to 49: 73%
50 to 64: 63%
65+: 56%

Location
Urban: 71%
Suburban: 72%
Rural: 69%

Income
>$75k: 72%
$50k to $75k: 74%
$30k to $49k: 69%

<$30k: 77%

Education
College Graduate: 74%
Some College: 71%
High School or Less: 70%

Facebook is one social media network that nearly everyone is on and not only that, but it carried a variety of different content on its server. You can post photos, text posts, share articles, and post videos. There isn't much that you can't do, and there isn't a lot of niches that don't have a place somewhere on the platform. Hence, yes, Facebook is definitely a must, but it's not necessarily a ride-or-die. There are plenty of brands who just fine without a Facebook account.

Instagram

Instagram is valuable in two ways: one is that it's very widely global, and two, it's very visual. That means that if you have a business that is all about visuals, this one's for you. If you can make a product look very visually pleasing or your niche relates to visually pleasing things. Also, if you're a business with international reach, 70% of Instagram's 1 billion users are from outside of the USA. Not only that but the average Instagram user spends a lot of time on the app, over 20 minutes a day. Considering the fact that Instagram is pretty much all about visuals and pictures, this is pretty impressive.

Not only that, but Instagram is pretty much all about selling. As bad as this sounds, it's true. 1 in 3 Instagram users has said that they use the platform to look for new products. Not only that, Instagram influencers, people who post pictures on the platform with products for money, can make thousands of dollars by simply talking about products.

One of the biggest things to know about Instagram is that engagement is key. Engagement is the one way to grow, so it requires constant attention throughout the day. It's not just that, but you definitely need an artistic eye to make the most of it. If you feel you can do that, read below for the demographics.

Gender
Men: 22%
Women: 29%

Age
18 to 29: 53%
30 to 49: 25%
50 to 64: 11%
65+: 6%

Location
Urban: 28%
Suburban: 26%
Rural: 19%

Income
>$75k: 26%

$50k to $75k: 26%
$30k to $49k: 23%
<$30k: 28%

Education
College Graduate: 24%
Some College: 31%
High School or Less: 33%

As you can see, Instagram is especially popular with the younger generation, and not so much with the older generation. Over the past few years, there has definitely been a shift where the younger generation has gone towards this more. Instagram even saved itself with the introduction of its stories feature a few years back, and its user base has exploded. It only hit 1 billion users this past year, and that number will only keep growing.

YouTube

I am not really going to talk about the demographics of YouTube, mostly because there isn't really a demographic of YouTube. YouTube is basically based around video content, with very little wiggle room. There isn't really a group of people who don't use YouTube. Not only that, but it's the number 1 place that people go online for video content, despite the fact that other websites such as Facebook and Twitter and Instagram have made it easier to share. Nothing can beat YouTube, and it's likely not going to lose its throne, or any of its 1.6 billion users anytime soon.

Basically, if your content is very video-based, YouTube is the place for you. It also requires a lot of work to upkeep and is much more skill-based than other platforms. However, it's also a great way to reach a huge group of people. If you're willing to put in the work and be consistent, YouTube is definitely the place to be. It's also great if you want to show off skills or products, giving your followers a taste of what your products will give them.

Twitter

Twitter is all about the quick and the fast and the short. If there is a thought that is 260 characters or less, Twitter is where you will find it. Twitter, similar to Instagram, is also incredibly worldwide. 80% of its user base is international.

Twitter is also incredibly popular for journalist and news, considering that it's all about what's in the now. News is often broken on the platform. Not only that, but Twitter is actually the originator of customer service through social media. It's the place where people would go to communicate with their favorite brands and celebrities directly. With 270 million active users, the average Twitter user will follow 5 or more businesses that they like, and a third of them (about 37%) of them will buy from a business through Twitter.

It's not only that, but Twitter is the perfect place to really add some personality into your brand in the form of 260 characters. Words are pretty powerful, and Twitter is the one place that proves that. If you're still not sure if Twitter is the fit for you, check out these demographics:

Gender
Men: 24%
Women: 21%
Age
18 to 29: 37%
30 to 49: 25%
50 to 64: 12%
65+: 10%

Location
Urban: 25%
Suburban: 23%
Rural: 17%

Income
>$75k: 27%
$50k to $75k: 27%
$30k to $49k: 21%
<$30k: 20%

Education
College Graduate: 30%
Some College: 24%
High School or Less: 16%

Twitter is definitely one of these places to go if you really feel that you have something to say. The platform also depends heavily upon words and instant. You need to address something quickly, and pretty much be on the platform all day. The average brand on Twitter does post about an average of 8 times a day throughout the day. Of course, there are ways to make this easier on yourself, but it can be a bit of a slog, at least when you're still getting used to it.

And that's what we got as to what you're going to need, and where you should be. Now, we're going to go through each of the social media networks mentioned in this chapter. We'll go over what they can do, how you can use them effectively, and how to grow your following so you'll see an increase in profit. Carry on.

CHAPTER 3: USING FACEBOOK WITHOUT MONEY

If you're going to be using Facebook, congratulations—there are some genuinely good reasons to use Facebook, and it's not just because of its huge user base, which spans the globe. Facebook has come a long way since its creation in Mark Zuckerberg's Harvard dorm room. Now, it's the number one social media network used by businesses world-wide, and it should be the one for you as well.

There are plenty of things that can be done on social media that definitely could not be done in the early days, with a huge variety of different content published on the platform. It's not just you can do a lot with the platform. Facebook is pretty much what brought social media into the mainstream, thanks to the fact that it was easy to adapt. When it first came onto the scene, it had fierce competition from Myspace, which was the most popular social media network at the time.

Why did Facebook succeed over Myspace? Myspace is now a network that is pretty much dead, and while it's still there, it's seen as mostly a place to go to discover music (believe it or not) rather than a real social media network. It's pretty much forgotten. Hence, why did this happen? Well, the quick answer is, Facebook adapted. Myspace didn't. And this is still a major part of Facebook's success. It adapts. It sees what's working and what isn't working and quickly does what needs to be done. If they see something that is working on another network, they work quickly to get it on theirs. It has the big advantage to its huge user base. If Facebook provides something on it, what's the point of moving onto another network? There isn't one.

For a lot of people, Facebook accounts for most of their internet usage, basically just using Facebook and Google. Considering that Google is the only website that outranks Facebook in terms of visitors per year, this is hardly surprising. The average amount of time its daily users spend on it 40 minutes every day. For some people, they don't even use any other social media network, especially the older generation.

Here are some other stats you should probably know:

- 85% of Facebook's Daily Users come from outside of the USA. Facebook is more than just the USA, with a huge International base (it is banned in several countries, including China). Over 80% of the interactions on the site come from outside of the USA as well, with India, Brazil, and Indonesia with the highest user base after the USA.
- More than 70 translations are available on the platform. With such an international audience, it makes sense that Facebook would let members translate with ease on the platform. More than 300,000 people have helped with the translation at the time of this being written. This is something that people with

brands who want to reach an international audience want to take into consideration. Being able to reach people through languages is a valuable skill to have, and makes it easier for people who may not necessarily know about your content find your content.

- There are more than 60 million businesses have a Facebook Page, while 60% of users follow Facebook pages. One-third of Facebook users actually engage with brands regularly, resulting in about 5 billion Facebook comments being made specifically on Facebook business pages monthly. All of these stats prove that Facebook is a valuable tool, and can be used to really help your business.

- The average person on Facebook checks their Facebook about 8 times per day. While people use their Facebook messenger apps an average of 3 times per day. With people on the platform about 40 minutes per day, which may not seem like much, but keep in mind that they're checking it a lot. What this information can tell you is that you should be scheduling your posts throughout the day. Most businesses post about 3 to 8 times a day, throughout the day, because of this.

- 400 users sign up for Facebook every minute. Within this minute, there are also 317,000 new status updates, 147,000 photos uploaded, and 54,000 shared links. This means that Facebook is still growing, and it's still being used. It's truly the biggest social media network out there on the planet, and that's not going away anytime soon.

- 19% of time spent on Facebook is through the mobile app or a mobile internet app. Facebook is one of the biggest reasons people spend time on their phone, with the average person spending about 5 hours a day on their personal mobile device. This is important to remember when you're making your posts. If people are consuming a lot of Facebook on their mobile phones, it makes sense that you should be making your posts smartphone friendly.

- On Facebook, there are 8 billion views on videos. Using videos on the platform isn't a bad idea, especially if you plan on having very visual based content. While Facebook hasn't beaten out YouTube in terms of video content, it's still a pretty strong contender. Also, people are much more likely to watch Facebook videos from their phones, so be sure to keep that in mind as well.

And these are the stats that you should know because they'll help you decide what kind of content you plan on posting. These stats, plus the age demographics we mentioned in Chapter 2, will help you come up with your strategy.

Now, we're going to talk about everything that you need to become a master Facebook user. Not only that, but this chapter is all about things that you can do that will cost you absolutely nothing, just your time. It may take a few hours a day, but the profits that you see that are a direct reward thanks to your efforts will be worth it. Hence, we're going to talk about the different kinds of Facebook posts, how to grow organically, and more.

Types of Facebook Posts

We've already talked a bit about just the huge variety of posts that Facebook has. I think it's important to know what these features are and what kind of content you should be sharing with them. Also, keep in mind, considering that Facebook is constantly updating just what kind of posts they can do, there will probably be a bunch more added before the year is halfway through.

- Text: this is what you think of when you think of a Facebook status. This isn't a particularly popular one used by marketers, as studies have been done to prove that a text post doesn't get anywhere near the amount of engagement that visual media does. However, it's still valuable, and plenty of conversations can be started up this way. Even just use it to update people as to what's going on in your business.

- Photos: whether or not you like to use photos, you should still do it. Photos just get more engagement across the board, and there's a reason why networks such as Instagram and Snapchat are so popular because they're completely image based. People love nice pictures, and they're more likely to get shared and commented on, boosting their impact. You don't even have to use your own pictures: even just stock images are OK, or a quote picture.

- Videos: the type of marketing that gets the most engagement is video marketing, no doubt about it.

There is a reason why YouTube is the third most popular website that's used online, only outdone by Facebook and Google. Even a thirty-second video showing off a product will work wonders.

- Pinned: this tool is pretty simple. It lets you take a post and "pin" it to the top of your profile. This makes it the first post that someone will see when they click onto the page, and it's a useful tool if you have something that is really important that people need to know.

- Links: this one makes it easier for you. Not all of the content that you share has to be yours, but it does need to have something to do with your brand. It's showing your fans that you have your ear to the ground and you know what you're talking about. You're not just stuck in your own little bubble.

Tips on Building Your Profile

Knowing how to build your Facebook business page is really crucial. This guide will take you through it one step at a time. Your profile has to hit every ball out of the park. You need to prove what you stand for, what you do, and everything else. It needs to be perfect. You probably won't build the perfect profile right away, and you will definitely be tweaking it over and over again. That's just how it is, especially as your business changes. Hence, do expect to come back over and over again.

Hence, let's get started;

1. Pick your option. Facebook gives you six different options for what kind of page you get to pick from. Basically, what kind of business you are. This is very helpful, as it means that you will be able to generate likes and follows from the people you actually want to hear from. It narrows down the field of which you're picked from. You get the following options: company, local business/place, company, brand/product, entertainment, or cause/community. Just pick the one that fits your business or brand the best.

2. Take advantage of their customizable URL. After creating a Facebook business page, you automatically receive a URL. It's just a random batch of numbers spit out by the network. By customizing your URL, you're making it easier for people to find you, and it makes you appear more professional, lending strength to your brand.

3. Fill out your whole profile. Don't leave anything out; there shouldn't be any gaps in information. The bio, profile picture, cover photo, and everything else, it should all be there. Don't forget to keep updating these things regularly. You don't want your page ever to reflect information that is no longer true.

4. Choose your words carefully in your about us section. When people search you on Google, and your page comes up, the first 155 words of this will show up on it. Use targeted keywords, as many as you can make sound natural, and be sure that those first 155

characters reflect your brand well. Adequately putting forward your mission statement is important here.

5. Use keywords. We just mentioned keywords, but keywords truly are essential to use. They make it easier to find you through search engines, both Facebook's own search bar and others like Google and Bing. Use them liberally, in both the about us section and the posts you make.

6. Get used to and explore all of their features. Facebook has so many features, and you definitely won't be using all of them constantly. But because they're always adding more to the platform, it can get really easy to just not even bother. You should be checking them out because they may be useful to your brand. Even when you get on now, there are a ton of features that haven't been tested by too many brands. Lead the pack. Be the one that tries it out. A lot of them have been ignored, which is a shame. Not only that, but it makes you a true master.

7. Last but not least, you need to start releasing valuable content. Content that is valuable not only to your business, but also your followers. You can do all of the above tips, but if your content is not great, you will not get anywhere. Put thought into your content. Always be sure that it is important and informative to your audience. Always talk to your audience like you would a friend. Be personal. Just keep doing these things, plus follow all the tips in our next section, and you should grow like wildfire.

Tips on Growing Organically

Yes, posting quality content is important. Being sure to be personal with your followers is important. But there are other things that you can do to obtain more followers, and all of these tips will help you do it. The most important thing to remember about growing on any social media site is engagement. Traffic. Likes, comments, and shares. It's the most important thing to remember as you head into the world of social media as we talked about a bit before.

Hence, what exactly is growing organically? Organically growing is when you grow without any help from ads or other paid means. We are going to talk a bit about ads in the next chapter and how to use Facebook ads to the best of their ability, but for now, we're going to talk about all the things you can do to get followers without spending any of your hard earned dollars.

Also, let's be honest. Organic reach can be tough on Facebook. It's just a fact, and the website is known for it. The reach has definitely declined in the last few years. This boils down to two separate issues. One, more content is being published than there is news space. Every month, 30 billion posts get published on Facebook. That's a whole lot, and it clogs up the newsfeed pretty easily. Second, Facebook will only show relevant content to each separate user. Just because someone likes your page, that doesn't mean that people are going to see your posts, unfortunately. Remember, there is already a ton of information being thrown at them, and Facebook will pretty much only show them the stuff that they know they're interested in. This is based on a variety of things.

The question remains, can businesses fight this? The answer? Of course.

You may think after reading that organic reach is declining, that you should jump immediately to our ad section. Well, this isn't the case. In fact, you should care. For starters, organic reach is better at actually starting conversations.

People like to ignore ads. That's just reality. If we can ignore ads, we will. We may not be able to escape their influence completely, that's just facts, but if we can, we do. I'm not saying that ads won't work, but I am saying that if people can find you organically, that's just better for your business.

Another thing to consider is the fact that there is no guarantee that Facebook ads are going to work. I would always recommend building up your following organically, figuring out what works, and using that knowledge to build your ad campaign. If you're already a marketing expert with advertising experience, you probably already know what works, but if you're not, it's different. Figure out what works first with organic reach, and use that knowledge before you throw any money at something.

Hence, here is a long list of different things you can do to build your organic reach and hit the social media height of your dreams.

1. Don't just post things to do with your business. I know what you're thinking, what's the point of having a profile for my business if I don't just post stuff from mine? Well, for starters, it's boring. Huge chain brands can get away with this a bit more than smaller businesses. In general, it's just not fun and feels like your entire page is an ad. Technically, you can see it this way, but you'll likely get more results if you talk about something else other than just selling to them or promoting your own content and products. Hence, talk about other things within your niche. Are you a local farmer? Talk about the products you use on your plants. Are you a local store? Mention how there is a great article on supporting local businesses. This starts conversations with your audience, and people will follow you and support you because of this.

2. Customize your page as much as possible. We already talked about building your profile, but that was pretty basic stuff. You can add customizations to your page, like tabs, email forms, podcasts, video players, quizzes, polls, landing pages, blog feeds, and so much more.

3. Link your other social media platforms on the network. I don't know you, but if you built a sizable following on another platform, be sure to let them know that you have a Facebook account.

4. Remind followers to turn on notifications for posting. Facebook allows users to get notified every time their favorite brand posts, so be sure to let them know

about it. If you have a great relationship with your followers and they love your content, this is more likely to work.

5. Use solid visuals. Visuals are really the best way to get engagement on Facebook, whether it's through video or pictures. Make sure that all the pictures really reflect what your company is about, and make it look good. Check out Instagram's chapter and YouTube's chapter for more tips on both of these mediums.

6. Don't be too formal. Remember, your followers are people too. Social media has created this unique relationship that you really need to take advantage of where brands can humanize themselves. Do this; it works.

7. Don't waste too much on words. People don't want to read giant blocks of texts. Keep your status updates short and snappy, and if you need to write a big block of text, be sure to space them out so that they're easier to read.

8. Use call to actions. Call to actions are statements like "sign up now!" "click here!" "get it now!", ones like that. It's a simple way to get more engagement and actually works with upping your results.

9. Create an invite-only Facebook group for your special audience members. If you have a solid group of people that you're always talking to and people who are always heading to your page for like and comment on things, then make a group with them. Facebook is all about building communities, and making

a group is an easy way to do just that. You can talk and engage with the people who advocate for your brand. Start a group around anything, from your brand, a specific product, a lifestyle, or specific topics. You don't even have to start a group for your customers; you can start one all about your niche. Just as long as you can rally a bunch of people around a specific topic or common goal, you've got your group. To be clear, a group specifically around a brand or product seems to work best, as you can hold Q&A's, coaching sessions, personal implementation feedback sessions, and be accountable. It helps encourage success and customer loyalty. Just be sure to set some rules and only invite people into the group who you know really love your products.

10. Target your posts. Targeting is definitely not just limited to Facebook ads; you can do it with posts as well. It can be based around the time of day (when it posts and when it stops showing up in people's newsfeed), you can serve the post to customers based on their age, gender, education, or location. You can enable targeting by going to your page settings, under general.

11. Consider timing. There isn't really just one answer in terms of "what time should I post?" People like to think that there is, there isn't. There are so many things to consider, like where your audience is located, the type of content you create, your audience's lifestyle, and so much more. The time that seems to work best for most marketers is between 1 and 4 PM,

but just because it's your 1 PM doesn't mean that it's your audience's 1 PM. My recommendation is to, instead of sticking to just posting at one time per day, time your posts so that they filter through throughout the day. There's more chance that everyone sees your posts this way.

12. Mix it up a bit. Facebook users want to see some variety from their favorite brands. This means posting a mix of text posts, photos, videos, links, and more. Mix it up, and take advantage of all of Facebook's posting features. There are some pretty great ones.

13. Post frequently, but test out what works for you. How much a business page posts really depends on them. For example, websites like Huffington Post and The New York Times are constantly posting content every day, pushing it on Facebook. Sometimes, they'll post up to 20 times in one day. For you, this may not be realistic. These companies have huge marketing branches behind them, and someone is hired to do that, all day. How much you post really comes down to your amount of followers and how often you actually have to do it. Be warned—there are actually risks of losing followers if you post too often, so you should probably start off with 1 to 5 posts a day at first. You can work up to more if you really feel it's necessary. You don't want to overwhelm your audience and clog up their newsfeed; they won't like that.

14. Work with other Facebook pages. Collaborations work. That's just how it is. It's done on both Instagram and YouTube constantly and giving shoutouts all the time on it. You can offer shoutout deals on Facebook, or share other business's products. It helps to increase the engagement and traffic to each page, and it also shows that there is a friendly competition between everyone. Reach out to other pages and businesses in your niche and share posts from each other's websites, give each other shoutouts, and even do product collaborations together. There are no limits to what you can do.

15. Run contests. One of the easiest ways to increase your presence on Facebook, making contests are also a fun way to bond with your fans. You can do so many things with a contest, grow your fan base, increase engagement, and generate more leads. There are several different kinds of contests you can run, but one the easiest ones are making a post, asking a question to answer in the comments plus tagging a friend the comment. Be sure to check out Facebook's rules for running a contest.

16. Let your friends know. You likely already have a Facebook profile, and if you're an avid user, you could have up to thousands of friends. Simply let them know that you've created the page. They're likely to follow and like it because they like you. Friends support friends, after all.

17. Be different. We've all been told that being different is a good thing, and on social media, that's no different. Find your differentiating factor, and show it off all over your page. Everything should stand out. One of the easiest ways to do this is with colors. Avoid blues, whites, and grays. Blue, white, and gray are Facebook colors, so it's going to be hard to stick out in their newsfeed if you use them. It doesn't even just need to be the whole post; even just highlights will draw the eye. Bright colors especially, considering that Facebook's colors aren't eye-catching.

18. Use all of Facebook's features. We've already talked a bit about the basic types of posts that Facebook has. I didn't put this above, because for me these are more features than post types. It's easy for these features to fall under the radar because Facebook just has so many of them. Get familiar with them and really just try new ones as they come out.

    a. Facebook messenger bots. Yes, you can do marketing through messenger now. You can engage users and use targeted sequences to persuade them.

    b. 360-degree videos and photos. With this, you can capture a 360 panoramic view. You can showcase events, workspaces, groups, stores, and so much more.

    c. Autoplay video. No longer do users have to tap on a video to play it; now as they scroll through their newsfeed, it just starts playing (this is a good reason to have captions on your videos).

Not only that but now you can watch videos as you're scrolling through, with a small window opening to the side of the screen, showing the video.

d. Facebook stories. Anyone who is familiar with Instagram or even Snapchat will know what these are. A video or photo that is posted and disappears under 24 hours. This isn't available for Facebook business pages, but it may very well be added soon, so be aware.

e. Facebook offers. On Facebook, you can share coupons, discounts, and other promotional offers. You can create them alongside ad campaigns, but not necessarily.

19. Pay attention to your followers. This is a no brainer, but actually be sure to reply to concerns, comments, messaging. This will show that you're not just doing this to get followers but to provide a service. You're not just after the comments and the likes and the ego boost. You're there to listen to your followers.

20. Focus on Value. Value is what's going to keep your followers coming back, and which will keep them actually there. Take your mind off the numbers, and really put effort into your content. This is what will, at the end of the day, make people want to follow you. Share posts with objectives and make sure that they all provide value.

In conclusion, there is so much you can do with Facebook. So much, you're not ever going to hit all the bases. There's always going to be new content, new things to do, new people on it every day, and there is no way that there is going to ever be a time on Facebook when it's perfect. There's always going to be new things added to it. There is absolutely no ending in sight, and we wouldn't want it that way anyway.

Now, this chapter was all about talking about Facebook and how you can use it without spending money. Social media is beneficial in that you don't need to spend money, but there is no issue with having a bit of a boost on it. Facebook ads are great for businesses as they're cheap and they work. Hence, next chapter, we're going to talk all about Facebook ads and how to use them effectively. Hence, read on.

CHAPTER 4: FACEBOOK WITH MONEY

Advertising is often considered essential in running a business. You have to get the word out there. You have to let people know what you're doing. You have to be willing to stand up on top of the tallest mountain and scream out into the void so you can get your first paying customer.

Social media and Facebook has changed this slightly. You don't need to spend money on advertising on social media. It's not 100% necessary. You can get by without it. However, it doesn't hurt to have a little bit of a boost. There are definitely some benefits to it.

One of the keys to Facebook's huge growth has been their advertising platform. On the platform, marketers are known to spend billions of dollars to get their message out to their chosen audience. It's low cost, there are a lot of users, and it's just really appealing to any business, no matter how big you are. All of the biggest businesses and companies in the world use Facebook advertising; it's considered a staple in today's ad climate.

These stats may shed some light on just how much Facebook's advertising platform affects the world and why you should be using it:

- 93% of Marketers use Facebook advertising. Basically, there aren't too many people who are in the business of social media that aren't using Facebook ads to help them out a bit. That should speak for itself; it works for them, why not you?
- 3 million businesses use Facebook to market their business. 70% of them are not in the USA. This is hardly surprising considering that Facebook has such a huge global audience. This stat makes Facebook the most popular social media used for advertising. The next one on the list is Instagram, with 24%. However, considering the fact that Instagram is owned by Facebook, this basically just means that the majority of these advertisers got their ads on Instagram through Facebook.
- Images have the highest effectiveness out of all the Facebook advertising options, accounting for 75% to 90% of its performance. For titles, the most effective length is four words, with 15 words making up the link description. Hence, a picture with a 4-word title and a 15-word caption would metaphorically get the most engagement. You can say a lot with just that.
- The average CPC (Cost Per Click) for Facebook ads is $1.72. Are you paying too much for your Facebook ads? Well, here's an easy way to figure it out. If you find that your cost is significantly higher than the average, try making some tweaks to your campaign.
- Organic Reach for a branded Facebook page is very low, at 2%. Yes, you can reach an audience without ads, but it's very much an uphill battle. It's just not

what it used to be. The above 2% number is just an average, so there are a lot of pages out there whose organic reach is much lower.

That last one is the most likely one that's going to drive you to the advertising, but it can still absolutely feel like a huge job. You're probably wondering if it's actually in your ability to do so. Well, I'm here to tell you that absolutely it is.

Facebook Ads is a great place to advertise your business and an exceptional system. And it's hard not to feel a bit overwhelmed, especially when you consider how massive the platform is. And when you do research, you just end up being more overwhelmed, and you just don't do it. Well, you're in luck. In this section, we're going to talk all about Facebook ads. We're going to get in deep how to do it, what kind of ads you can choose from, and hopefully answer any questions you might have.

Not only that, but the advantages of Facebook ads are a lot more than just these above stats. There are a ton of other amazing features that they have. They offer full creative control over your ads—you're able to target them completely, and more. Not only that, but Facebook ads are directly intertwined with Instagram ads. You can run ads on both of the platforms in a single campaign, meaning that you can hit two birds with one stone. This is a brilliant advantage if you want to reach as many people as possible.

And best of all about Facebook ads? They're made for small businesses. Meaning, they're affordable. Now, let's get down to business.

Your Guide to Facebook Ads

Coming out with a winning advertising strategy seems like a complicated process, but it's really not. Facebook really tries to make it as seamless as possible, without a whole lot of confusion. They walk you through everything because they understand that there is a big chance that the person creating the campaign has never done it before. Their goal is to make it easy for you. With their help, and the help of this book, it will be easy, and you'll breeze right through it.

1. Develop your strategy first. The first step to any ad campaign, before you even look into Ads Manager, you need a strategy. This is something that every marketer does, regardless whether it's traditional ad marketing or social media marketing. If you don't do this, you'll just wind up creating a campaign that just doesn't do anything that you want it to. You just

won't get anywhere. Hence, before you even start to think about looking at ads manager, you need to do this; sit down with a piece of paper and write down the answers to the following questions:

a. What product or service do I want to promote?
b. Who is the person I am targeting? What is their age, their sex, their location, their relationship status, etc.?
c. How will they use the product? How will it help their life?
d. What objectives will they have to the product? What are the possible complaints that will arise?
e. What is the goal of the campaign? Do I want brand awareness, site traffic, sales, leads, or something else?
f. If there is not a strategy, if you don't know what goals you have and what you want to accomplish, then your campaign will fail. Hence, take your time, and make a game plan. It will help you out so much in the future.

2. Choose your objective. The first step to creating a campaign is to choose an objective, and you have to choose the right one. This is something that Facebook needs to know so your campaign will work on their server. It will help them optimize ad placements, all based on what your objective is. This will improve the results of your campaign. On Facebook,

there are 11 different objectives you can choose from:

g. Reach
h. Brand awareness
i. Engagement
j. Traffic
k. App Installs
l. Messages
m. Video views
n. Lead generation
o. Conversions
p. Catalog Sales
q. Store Visits

It's important that your objective doesn't just fall in with your short term goals, but your long term goals as well. Your objective should add to your overall version. Every campaign you run will have something to do with the other. Of course, testing out different objectives is never a bad thing. In fact, it's a good thing. Remember, testing and weighing things out is the best way to figure out what works for you and your page. You're definitely not going to get everything right on the first try, so testing out your options will help. You're not just limited to one campaign.

3. Target your audience. You likely already know who you want to sell to, but this is where you really flesh it out. Facebook allows you to be extremely specific

when it comes to picking your audience, and there are several options you can choose.

r. Custom audience: this targets people who have already taken an interest in you, whether it's subscribing from your email list or spending time on your websites or Facebook/Instagram profile. People who may just need a bit of an extra boost.

s. Lookalike audiences: this one takes your current audience, takes notes of the demographic qualities they have such as age, gender, and more, and aims the content at people who match up.

t. Demographic targeting

u. Location targeting

v. Interest/behavior targeting

w. Connection targeting: this one determines whether or not you want to show ads to users who are not or are connected to your brand.

4. Choose where you want your ad to be shown. There are plenty of options as to exactly where your ads will be shown, and Facebook has seemingly managed to squeeze ads in every crevice of the website. You can choose for your ads to only appear through desktop, but you can also choose for them to only appear on mobile. You can also pick both. There's also all of the options of where on Facebook you want them to be, and options for Instagram as well. You can pretty much run any ad with almost all of

the placement options (the one left out of this is Instagram story ads; you can only use that placement). You can disable or enable certain ones you want to choose from. It really all depends on you and your business. Here are all of the Facebook ad placement options:

x. Facebook feeds: it shows in user feeds, mostly pictures, single images, or carousel ads.
y. Facebook Instant articles: shows an article, and is mobile only.
z. In-Stream Video: these play before, during, and after a video is played. They're very brief, usually 10 seconds or less.
aa. Right column. Nondescript, and appear on the ride hand side of the feed. It's desktop only and has disadvantages in that it has limited text and isn't in a user's line of site.
bb. Suggested Videos: Facebook suggests the video after a user has watched a video. It's available on both mobile and desktop, but you can only use it for brand awareness, app installs, video views, and post engagement.
cc. Instagram Feeds: Video, image, and Carousel ad formats can be shown in your Instagram feed (mobile only).
dd. Instagram stories: shows up between Instagram's stories.

ee. Facebook Messenger Home. Ads will be displayed on Messenger's home screen. This ad format is still being tested out—mobile only.

ff. Messenger Sponsored: ads being delivered right to a user's phone as a personal message, with a CTA at the bottom. They will, of course, be labeled as sponsored and will show up in both messenger mobile app and the desktop version.

5. Set a budget. In this stage of Facebook ads, you can choose your budget, schedule your ads, and set your optimization method. Daily budget or lifetime budget? Will your ads run indefinitely or be scheduled to start and end on certain dates? If you want your ads to only run certain times of the day or times of the week, use a feature called dayparting. You can also choose to optimize your ads, which you may be a bit wary of. Facebook automatically sets things up for you, so you don't have to update them manually. You should only be manually updating them if you're familiar with the system and there is a good reason for doing so. Basically, this stage, you can choose how fast you want your ad budget to be spent, and you can set a cap on your bids. You can even choose to change what you're bidding on. Take some time to adjust to and get used to this stage.

6. Choose the ad format you want. This personally is my favorite state of the game, as Facebook has so many great and powerful ad formats. They all do great. What you choose will depend on what you

want out of them, as different ads tend to have different results. You can choose from the following:

gg. Single Image Ads: just a simple single image.
hh. Video Ads: a video, usually 60 seconds or less. The length also depends on where the ad will be located.
ii. Carousel Ads: think a long stream of images that a consumer can flip through looking
jj. Canvas Ads: this is a full-screen ad, and usually works best on mobile.
kk. Collections: a collection of photographs where a user can scroll through

There is no advertisement here that doesn't have its benefits. Facebook really strives to provide a wide variety of ad formats, so there isn't a business out there that feels like their needs aren't being met. This means that they'll likely ad more options in the future. Actually, it's pretty much guaranteed.

7. Get the details down. Details are easy to miss in a lot of situations, and Facebook's ad manager is no different. These little details are located at the very bottom of the entire page. There are things like CTAs and URL descriptions, which you may not think about if it wasn't there. You should be taking your chance to examine and play with every one of them. The CTA button will help better your conversion rates, and using the right copy in the right place could

make or break your campaign. You will see the difference between a campaign that uses this section and one that didn't.

8. Pay attention to your ads, carefully. It can be easy to just fall into a habit of not monitoring your ads once they're out there. After all, the job is done, why not just let them do the work for you? This is a mistake because by monitoring your ads you'll be able to learn valuable information that will help you create better campaigns in the future. You'll be able to see all of the active details of your campaign, including CPC, frequency, relevant scores, and numbers of actions. These numbers are crucial and will help you narrow down what's working so your next ad campaign will be even better.

I think that you'll find that Facebook ads will work for you. It may be a bit complicated at first, with all of the options to choose from (there are quite a lot). Advertising is tricky no matter how old you are if you're new to it. But this will work to your advantage rather than your downfall. As long as you stick to the process we just outlined, and make sure that you're keeping with the program, you'll do fine. You just need to have an iron-clad, thought-out plan before you head in, which will make the campaign process run so much easier. This will lead to much stronger and better ads, and you'll get more results.

That's pretty much all we have to say about Facebook ads in this chapter. Now, for the next chapter, we're going to get into Facebook's cousin, Instagram, the social media network built entirely on photographs and videos. Just visual content, which some may brush off but it's pretty powerful. Remember, Facebook and Instagram are run by the same company, so all the information in this chapter also applies to Instagram. This just makes it easier for you. Bonus; that's not the only place where Instagram and Facebook are totally in sync. Read on.

CHAPTER 5: INSTAGRAM 2020

Think about it—Instagram is entirely built off on images.

When Instagram was first released in 2010, nobody could have predicted just how well it actually would do. The idea of a social media platform just built off of images was laughable. Up until then, most social media networks had multiple forms of posting, such as images, videos, and text posts. Instagram put all of their better on just one—visual— and it paid off.

Now, Instagram is one of the biggest social media networks in the world—outdone only by Facebook and YouTube. With it recently hitting its one-billion-user mark, there are no signs anywhere that Instagram is going to be slowing down anytime soon—and considering that Instagram was actually bought out by Facebook, there is no way that they're going to be slowing down. Slowing down just doesn't exist in Facebook's dictionary.

Instagram is the perfect place for marketers. It just is. Thanks to its image-based system, there is no time when you can't be showing off your products. It's the perfect place to really forward an image of what your brand is. Visual marketing is very powerful, so if you do have products or you're trying to sell a lifestyle, Instagram is the perfect place to do so.

Not only that but Instagram's user base alone makes it a worthwhile place to go. Just check out some of the insane stats about the platform here:

- It has 1 billion monthly users. They passed that goal in 2019. Over 60% of users do log in and check on it every day. This makes it the second most-engaged network after Facebook.
- 80% of Instagram users are from outside the USA. The top three countries that use Instagram are the USA, India, and Brazil. 35% of people who use the internet in the USA use Instagram.
- 90% of Instagram users are younger than 35.
- In June 2016, it was estimated that every day, 95 million posts are made every day. That number is likely to be far higher today. There are an estimated 3.5 billion likes made on the platform every day.
- Its usage has doubled since 2016.
- There are over 25m brand accounts on Instagram. 80% of users follow at least one brand account. If you look at the top 100 brands known in the USA, 90% of them have a brand account.
- 60% of Instagram users seek out and discover products on the platform. 1 in 3 has used Instagram directly to make a purchase.
- Engagement is the number one most important thing on Instagram, with the average post getting 10 times more engagement than the average Facebook post. It

also gets 84 times more engagement than the average Twitter post. The average amount of engagement on a post has gone up 416% in two years.

- Photos see more engagement on the platform than most videos. This may be surprising for a lot of people, but considering that Instagram is completely based around pictures, it really shouldn't be.

- 32% of teens name Instagram as their favorite social media network, and the one that they view as the most important. This is more than any other social media network, including Snapchat, which is often hailed as the one place to connect with teenagers.

With everyone now owning a smartphone with a camera, and now everyone thinking that they're suddenly a professional photographer, it's not actually a surprise just how much people have taken to Instagram.

Instagram isn't just a social media network though. Yes, it's a great place to keep track of what your friends are up to and no doubt a lot of people follow their friends on the platform. But you need to remember that what Instagram has turned into is a place to flex. To show off. To post pictures of your latest great adventure and prove how great your life is.

That's how you need to treat Instagram as a place to market. You need to show the lifestyle that your brand has. That's the biggest mistake I see a lot of businesses making in terms of Instagram. They just post pictures of their product with absolutely zero thought into "how is this product going to make my ideal customer feel?" Will they feel sexy? Funny? Sweet? Adventurous? Thrilled?

Just showing your audience a picture of a product won't cut it. You need to show them how they're going to feel. Take this for example:

Let's say you sell mountain climbing gear. Backpacks. Shorts. Tank tops. Comfortable hiking boots. Tents. Sleeping bags. Healthy, portable snacks you can eat while climbing. Wattle bottles. Whatever else you need for a hiking trip.

Well, what's more interesting, a simple picture of a tent, or a picture of that tent, set up with a fantastic view of mountains, and a person sitting outside eating one of these portable snacks? It's just more interesting.

To be fair, you can get results from the other option, just pictures of your products. And putting forward a completely well put-together image just may not work for you. Personally, I would recommend that you mix it up. Have pictures of products, but also mix them with pictures of your lifestyle.

That's only the first piece of advice I have for you in this chapter. In this chapter, we're going to talk about building your profile, what you can do to gain followers, how to post onto the platform effectively, and even a tiny bit about Instagram ads. Here we're going to build the perfect Instagram strategy, and how to sell on the platform. Let's get started.

Building Your Profile

Building your Instagram profile is a slightly different and more complicated ballgame than any other social media platform. On platforms like Twitter and Facebook, you depend on a combination of words and images to sell the platform. This means that while visuals are important, it's not nearly as important as on Instagram. On Instagram, all of your selling points rest on your images. And because when somebody taps on your profile and the first things they see is the last six to ten posts you've made, you need to make sure that every image is 100% cultivated perfectly. Every inch of your profile is a direct representation of your brand, which is why it's so essential that you put a lot of effort into it.

Hence, we're going to try and make this as easy for you as possible. In this section, we're going to go step by step in building your profile, from your profile picture to your bio to your first 10 or so pictures. It's all here.

First, let's talk about your username.

Your username should be as close as possible to your business's name. You want people to be able to find your ad as quickly, and as easily as possible, so your business's name should be number 1. If you can't make that work, as it may already be taken, consider finding a twist on it. For example, let's say there is a bakery called Betsy's Cupcakes who is looking for a username. If @betsyscupcakes doesn't work, try something like @betsys.cupcakes or @betsys_cupcakes. Avoid using too many periods or underscores though; it just doesn't look professional. If you can have just your name, do that.

Next thing we'll discuss is your title. Your profile title is more important than your username, in my opinion. You're still searchable on the platform with just that, so this should definitely just be your company's name. You have 30 characters in the title card, which should be plenty. One tip that works wonders is including exactly what you do in the title. For example, let's say there is a writer named Jennifer Stevens who wants to help sell her work by sharing writing tips online. Well, rather than just have the name "Jennifer Stevens," she'd instead write "Jennifer Stevens, Writer." This works wonders and would help her gain followers. This means that people who like to look at writing images look in the search for them, and then will find Jennifer directly. She may gain them as a follower just based on that.

Then, it's time to talk about your profile picture. Your profile picture is the tiniest picture that you will have on your profile, and since you can't actually enlarge it, a lot of people don't often think about it too much. This is a mistake. Think about it; your profile picture is the first thing that users will see of you, tiny or not. If you have a logo, this is where your logo should go. It's the perfect thing to use as a profile picture. If you don't have a logo, follow these tips:

- Something clear and concise. Just a picture of your smiling face really suffices. Portrait mode is probably the best bet for this kind of picture.

- Avoid a cluttered background. You don't want something in the background that will draw attention from the actual subject of the photograph. Just a plain background works just as well, preferably just one solid color. A background full of people is a definite no.

- Look nice. If it is going to be a photograph of yourself, be sure to look nice and professional. Like you actually know what you're doing. You don't want to say you know what you're doing in every other part of your profile, and not look the part in your profile picture.

Finally, it's time to talk about your bio.

Your bio will likely be one of the last things a potential follower will look at. This is likely because the eye will be automatically drawn to your images, and they'll read your bio second. However, your bio can also sell your profile. It can just add padding onto the vibe that a user is likely already getting just from looking at your photos. Most people don't know this, but your bio doesn't actually show up in search results. Meaning, you can fill it with as many keywords as you'd like, but no matter what, these keywords won't help people find you—which is why I really recommend following my advice about your title that I mentioned before. Having a solid bio is really important, and you need to fill it with as much information as possible before you can even post anything. Hence, follow the below tips to write a winning bio. You have 150 characters, so make sure you use them well.

- Use keywords. They may not help you with actually finding anything, but they will help you write your bio. Pick out two to three works that you want to write your bio around, and use these. Make sure they all have to do with what you are, what you do, and what your specialties are. However, really focus on the keywords that will capture your ideal follower's interests. What are their pain points? What do they want to see? What will resonate with them?

- Avoid full sentences. When you only have 150 characters, you don't need to be completely grammatically correct. You can get the point across in just a few words, rather than full, run on sentences. If you have to use full sentences, make sure they're short.

- Use emojis. For separating out these incorrect sentences, use emojis. It's a fun, playful way to do so that people like, and just looks good. If you don't want to use emojis, consider just spacing out your bio and add line break so that it's in list form. Just be sure to give your bio two enter spaces rather than one when your line breaks your bio.

- Put more than one link in your bio. Instagram only allows you to put in one link into your bio, and thankfully, there are ways to get around this. You simply just need to get a custom link, which takes a user to a webpage full of all the links that you may have mentioned. This means you can always say "link in my bio" in a post without having a swap it out every two days. Use a program like LinkTree to do so. If you don't want to use something like that, just simply put in a link to your website.

- Include your email address. If you are able to switch your account to a business profile, Instagram will let you put your email in automatically. If you don't want to have a business profile (it's really all up to you), you can simply put it in your bio. This is becoming more and more common for business owners and entrepreneurs.

- If you have a brand hashtag, use it here. Brand hashtags are specifically curated hashtags that companies use to communicate with their followers. One of the most iconic is Just Do It, by Nike. Nike uses this slogan for all of their campaigns, and type in #justdoit in the Instagram search bar, and you'll get 10s of millions of results of people doing sports. It's effective in getting people to stand up and actually post something to do with it. Include it in your bio, and people will get the message.

- Include a call to action. If you still don't know, a call to action is when you basically tell your followers to do something. Something like "subscribe here" or "like my latest post" or "check out my website." These are so simple but so effective.

- Include your physical location and hours. If you're a business that is based primarily in one area, then mentioning that is a must. Even just a shortened version of your city works well (using LA instead of Los Angeles). Including your business hours is also helpful to tourists who are looking for places to go to.

Use all these tips, and that should create an amazing bio for potential followers to read and enjoy. You don't need to make use of all the tips in this section, and you'll likely find yourself editing and redoing your bio thousands of times over the course of your Instagram career. It's part of life, and that's just how it is. It's never going to be perfect.

Next, we're going to talk about posting—and how you can post on Instagram effectively—that will get you the most engagement.

Doing up your bio is really barely half the bio. You're not going to get anywhere, on any social media network, unless you post. Posting is the backbone of any social media network, but on Instagram, it takes slightly more work. Mostly thanks to the fact that every image needs to look perfect and be beautiful to gain likes and follows. It needs to fit in with the rest of your brand.

You need to think of your Instagram page as almost like a collage of photographs. A collage of photographs needs to match up perfectly with each other. They need to look good at laying up against each other. Whether it's in terms of color, editing, or composition, sometimes all three, they need to match together. Basically, if the images don't look good up against each other, there's no point. It's not just that will help drive up your engagements. And that other thing is engagement.

Engagement is the number one thing to Instagram. It's the thing that will get you the most attention. It's the thing that will make sure you grow. You can't grow without optimal engagement. Pretty much all of the tips outlined in this entire chapter is all about you getting that engagement. Without it, your profile will fail. Hence, how do you get engagement? Well, first we're going to talk about posting, and what you can do to get optimal engagement. Then, we're going to throw out some basic tips that will up it a bit and some ideas on how to make it happen.

Hence, let's talk about posting.

First off, every single one of your pictures should have something to do with your niche. Personal photos should be only for personal accounts. If you want to post personal photos, you will lose followers. Look into any brand's Instagram page, and every single post will have something to do with their business, regardless of what the post actually is.

Secondly, you're going to need to have an aesthetic. What is an aesthetic? Well, an aesthetic kind of relates to the mood of your profile. How does your page make someone feel when they look at it? Happy? Sad? Excited? Inspired? Gloomy? The choice is yours. Each one of your pictures needs to relate back to this aesthetic easily; one easy way to do it is with color. Not only that, but this will also help you pick out your filtering and editing needs—which leads us to our next one.

Thirdly, all of your photos will have to be edited—and edited the same way. Remember how we talked about photo editing apps? You're going to need one here. Instagram does have its own editing functions on the app, but they don't look too great. Kind of cheap looking and the filters aren't the best. You want the best of the best.

Remember how your photos look up against each other. You want the photo collage effect, right? Hence, remember the photo collage. Editing your photos in the same and always having the same color scheme will definitely help you with this. Another way to make this a bit easier on yourself is by using an app called Preview. This app is specifically designed to help you build your Instagram feed into a literal collage. All it does is show you how your photos will look up against each other, and you can choose to edit and shuffle them around as you wish before it becomes a permanent part of your page.

And finally, the time of day really does count. There have been a lot of studies done on Instagram that shows there are certain times a day to post. However, the best times by far seem to be in the middle of the day. Typically, 9 to 5 working hours, ironically enough. When people are procrastinating on their phone at work—it happens. The afternoon, around 2 to 5, seems to be the absolute best time to post.

Here are some other lighting fast tips to follow to really encourage engagement when you post:

- Share your posts to your Facebook, Twitter, and even Tumblr if you have them. One of the best things about the fact that Instagram and Facebook are so connected is that you can easily link them and post easily to both of them.

- Write good captions with a call to actions. Be sure to let your personality fly through them, and if you want to write long ones, space them out. Followers are more likely to read them. Asking questions is also another way to encourage comments.

- Do post 1 to 2 times a day. Any more and people will unfollow you. If somebody follows 10 pages, they don't want just to see content from you. They want to see content from other accounts as well. Don't overwhelm them with content. 1 to 2 posts a day is plenty. If you want to post more, do it in stories, which we will be talking about in this next section.

- Before and after you post, like a bunch of photos in your niche. You should also only be following people who fall into your niche. For example, if you write poetry, all the accounts you should be following should have something to do with poetry in some form or another. However, right before you post, head into a hashtag having to do with your niche, and just like about 50 pictures. Then, after you've posted, go back into the hashtag, and like another 50. This will up the amount of engagement you receive. You should also be commenting on at least 10.

- Use hashtags. You get 30 hashtags per post, and you should be using them. If you don't like how they look, you can include them in the comments instead. It makes no difference as to how well your post will do.

- Reply and like comments on your page. It shows people that you're reading them, you're paying attention, and you acknowledge what they're saying, whether it's good or bad. Even just an emoji can speak volumes.

These are pretty much all the tips that will get you a lot of engagement. However, one other way of getting engagement is looked over a bit by brands in the social media community. And that's Instagram Stories. Let's talk about them.

When Instagram stories first came out, it was seen as this desperate attempt to profit off of Snapchat's ideas, basically just swiping the format from them. For those who don't know, stories are a post where it disappears after 24 hours, very similar to Snapchat's main and pretty much their only version of posts. Hence, when it first came out, a lot of people looked down on Instagram for pretty much just stealing the idea.

Needless to say, Instagram actually didn't need stories. It was doing just fine without the format. However, there's an argument to be made that Instagram may not have needed stories to continue succeeding, but it definitely helped rocket them into the huge platform that it is today. Thanks to the fact that Instagram became so much about showing off your life, people were only posting the best of the best to their profile. With stories, they could show both the great and perfect side, plus the not so perfect and put together side, through stories. Every day, over 300 million stories are posted on the platform. You could say that Instagram made a gamble, and it paid off.

Hence, how to post on stories, and what should you post?

One of the great things about stories it that it really helps add to the most humane side of your brand. You can show more personal and fun videos. The images can be shaky, and there just doesn't need to be that same level of perfection as there is in your regular posts. Here are some ideas that you can do:

- Touring around your workspace
- Interviews with employees
- Employee takeover (where one or more of your employees takes over your stories for a few hours/a day)
- Giving your followers coupons (they'll disappear after 24 hours!)
- Going live (take your followers on a journey live, and address issues in real time)
- Q and A (use the Q and A feature in the stickers section, and get people to send your questions
- Sneak peek your new products
- Doing a poll
- Countdown to new products; if there is something coming out or happening, do live countdowns to the time)

The real thing to remember about stories is that they're much more personal, and you can really have fun with them. They come with a ton of brilliant stickers. Here are just a few of your options;

- Gifs
- Filters
- Geotags

- Hashtags
- Music (only some regions)

You can also use video effects, such as Boomerang, Rewind, and Focus. These will give your videos some fun elements.

You should really be trying everything when it comes to stories. Try all of their features, and you can get some enjoyment out of them. There are plenty of cool effects that you can use, and no limit to the different ways of using them. Seriously, have some fun.

Instagram Ads

If you read our previous chapter on Facebook ads, you already know that Facebook and Instagram ads are very closely tied together. Facebook owns Instagram, so you actually need a Facebook business account to sign up for the ads. Why has Facebook chosen it to be this way? It's likely simply just to get more and more people to sign up for Facebook.

However, if you want to just have ads on Instagram, that is totally an option to do so. Here are some of the ad formats that Instagram supports:

Photo Ads: these allow you to showcase your product through a great image. Make sure it's the best of the best, and you'll get some likes and clicks. This is a great way to share a post with a larger platform of people.

Video Ads: Instagram users love video. You should be putting some videos in your feed anyway, which is why using them as ads is so powerful. If you ever decide to put together a full-length video ad, use it for Instagram ads.

Carousel Ads: an ad that lets you swipe through a series of images or videos, your choice. They offer the opportunity to create a story or highlight multiple products. Perfect for a brand who wants to show variety.

Stories Ads: these appear in between stories that users are already seeing. You can add face filters, video effects, and text, which makes room for more creative and interesting ads.

Canvas Story Ads: similar to Facebook Canvas ads, these are immersive video experiences, also between Instagram stories. You can create a custom canvas if you wish.

As we end this chapter, I'm just going to say this: Instagram is a powerful resource for a marketer, and you should be taking advantage of it. You can easily double or triple your following in just a few months if you really want to work at it, just by using these tips in here. However, I am going to leave you with one last piece of advice in regards to Instagram.

And it's simple: Don't. Buy. Followers.

It can be very tempting to do so but don't do it. It's bad for your account, and you could be classified as spam. You could actually lose your whole account, and be banned from the platform. It is 100% against Instagram's terms of service and is really just a cheap way to get followers. Not only that, but these followers won't be active. They're fake accounts, so nobody is behind them, making sure your posts actually get likes. They won't engage with your content. They won't buy anything. You'll have this massive high, and then be right back where you started, with no real change and no actual money coming through. It's better to have 100 real followers who will buy from you rather than 1,000,000 fake followers who'll just be sitting dead in your follower box. Remember that.

And, we have reached the end of this chapter. We've covered all of the basics of Instagram, and that's pretty much all there is to say on it. Next, we're going to be talking about the place where you go that has crazy amounts of video content. This platform may be the hardest one to master. And that's YouTube. We're going to talk about growing your subscribers, creating your profile, and ideas for videos. Then, we're going to get into its advertising. That's up next, and keep reading.

CHAPTER 6: YOUTUBE

YouTube is the largest video sharing website, hands down. There is no website online that can compete with it—or at least not one that you've heard of. It's the number one place that people go to get video content, and it has almost 2 billion users. That number keeps rising as more and more people get Google accounts, and that number doesn't even account for the people who go on and use the website without an account.

YouTube is a little underutilized by marketers. It's just not a platform that marketers think of when they think of a place where people will buy things. Yes, marketers may use YouTubers to promote content, but they'll rarely do it themselves.

But in reality, there is no person who isn't on YouTube. It's so diverse, and there is so much content on the website that there is no one person who cannot find something they're interested in on the network—which is why it's perfect for marketing. If you know you have content or products or service that appeals to a large demographic, why shouldn't you be on a website that appeals to the masses?

Here are just a few stats that YouTube brags of:

- 6 out of 10 internet users prefer online video content over regular service TV. This will be huge as time goes on, and fewer people pay for a subscribed TV service, instead choosing to get their entertainment online.
- 8 out of 10 18 to 49-year-olds watch YouTube in an average month. This is a huge demographic, and no other platform can brag these kinds of numbers. In 2015, for the same demographic, time on YouTube went up 74%. The time spent on YouTube has doubled in just the past year.

- YouTube has been launched in over 91 countries and is available in 80 different languages. It pretty much covers the entire Internet-using population.
- There are over 1 billion hours of YouTube videos watched every single day. This is more views than Facebook and Netflix combined.
- 70% of YouTube views come from mobile devices. On average, there are about 1 billion mobile video views each day.
- Only 9% of small businesses use YouTube. This could give you a huge advantage.
- Searches for "How to" videos go up for about 70% each year. This is especially important to know for marketers, as that gives you an immediate clue as to one of the many forms of video content you can make.

There aren't very many businesses out there who really invest in YouTube marketing. And this is hardly surprising, considering how much work it takes to really run a successful YouTube channel. I mean, think about it.

Compare a simple image and a full-scale video? There's no comparison. Videos even cost more to make. A simple three-minute video can cost up upwards of about $100 per video when your account for all the time, effort, and equipment required. The high stakes really scare people away from it.

However, it's still worth it. You just need to look at the stats above to prove that. Not only that, but it will give you a significant boost among your competitors. It gives you the option of really showing off what you can do and that you're in fact the best at it. In this chapter, I'm going to tell you how to do it. We're going to start with building your channel, planning your content, give you some ideas for videos, and really talk about how you can grow as a channel. Read on.

Creating Your Profile

The minute you create a Google account, you have a YouTube Channel. However, you're going to need a business channel if you want to make content. This is really easy to do, thankfully. All you have to do is follow these directions:

1. Log onto YouTube.com. Once you're logged in, there is a user icon at the top right of the screen.
2. Find a gear icon, which is settings. This will take you to a new page.
3. Once in settings, you can click on "Create New Channel."
4. There you'll find something called, "Use a business or other name." Just fill out your name.

And there you have it. Your YouTube channel is up and ready to start running.

Picking your brand name should be really simple; just the name of your business. This isn't a username, so there's no need for something really unique. If your business is already established, don't bother looking up online to see whether or not someone has it.

Now you can start filling out your profile. This is pretty easy too, and just follow this step by step process.

1. Fill out your "About Me" section. Here, do describe your business, the type of content you'll be creating, and links to other channels. Consider putting in your

business email address as well, so people can find you.

2. Put your channel art up. Your channel art is a large banner that sits at the top of your YouTube page, similar to a cover photo on Facebook or Twitter. You can put anything you like here, but what tends to work best is something done in the company colors with their name and a design that somehow represents what the company is. YouTube offers a template for those who are looking for inspiration. The proper size for this image is 2560 by 1440 pixels.

3. Choose your profile image. Similar to your channel art, this should also just represent who you are as a brand. Stick to your logo image or just a nice, clear, smiling photo of yourself.

And finally, you have your channel—all built up and ready to go. However, you won't get anywhere without content. So let's talk about that.

You should treat a YouTube strategy for content the same way you would treat a business strategy. Your content needs to be made for the people who you want to buy your products, so you need to make sure that your content specifically fulfills a need you have. The kind of content you make will really depend on that. It will also depend a lot on what kind of business you are.

For example, if you're an artist hoping to sell art classes, you'd probably do basic art tutorials online. This gives people a taste of what they can expect from you when they actually pay the full amount and come see you in class. It's also not giving them any more than what they'd already find online, in case you were worried about the fact that people would no longer pay for a service.

There is no shortage of video ideas out there. In fact, we're going to be listing a bunch for you pretty quickly here. But first, let's talk about the three golden steps to making quality content on YouTube:

It completely boils down to two reasons: entertain or accomplish. Either, they want to solve some kind of problem they're having, or they want just to shut their brain off and be entertained for a while. Your video needs to do one of these two things.

There is a crazy amount of content being uploaded to YouTube every minute. It's something like an average of 400 hours every single minute. And how a YouTube channel manages to really stick out is quality. The quality of content can make or break the success of a channel. There are plenty of channels out there who are putting out bad content; don't be one of them. It will get overlooked for the better-looking content, no matter how valuable your content is in terms of information.

I've heard having a successful YouTube channel is similar to having a successful TV show, and it's pretty accurate. You depend on your viewers, or in YouTube's case subscribers, to keep yourself going. But for the first bit, when you're not so successful, you need to keep going. Keep yourself on a schedule, and making regular videos. This means even when you're not feeling creative, you should still be putting out quality videos. This is why I've provided you the below list, so you'll never have to run out of video ideas.

Of course, you won't find that every single video on this list will work for you. Some of these are meant for different types of channels. Just circle the video ideas that appeal to you. As time goes on, you'll likely find it easier to come up with your own ideas as your channel has more of its own voice.

1. Introduce yourself. Describe yourself. Do a trailer for your channel where you talk about your brand, yourself, what you'll be talking about on it. You can pin it to the front page of your channel.
2. Respond to something. Is there an article in your business niche that was published? Is there a video made by a competitor that you have an opinion on? These are actually more likely to be seen than just random videos, so they're not a bad place to make a few at the beginning just to start off.
3. Vlog. There is plenty of different types of vlogs you can make. You can't do vlogs completely in the long run, but a vlog going behind the scenes, doing a tour of your workspace, or taking your viewers through a day in your company isn't a bad idea.
4. An opinion video. If you have an opinion about something relating to your business that is a bit of a hot button topic, post it. This will drive up comments

and engagement, helping bring more people to your channel.

5. Review something. This is how a lot of people sell things online. They build up their reputation by reviewing new products in their niche, anything from makeup to video editing apps, and before you know it, they're in a partnership making something or with an entire brand of their own. They do well because of the fact that their viewers already trust their opinion about certain products, so why wouldn't their own line of products be amazing?

6. Favorites. Do you have favorite things from your niche that your followers should know about? Tell them! It gives insight into where you get your information come or what helps you day-to-day.

7. Show off your products. If you have a new line of products coming out, or if you just want to show off your products anyway, just take your viewers through looking at them. Open the packaging, show off how they work, and tell them all about the manufacturing process.

8. Give advice in your niche. If you're someone trying to sell a service, like a course, there is no issue with giving people a bit of a peek at the good stuff. Just give a much shallower version than what you normally give, and make a case for them to buy your full course at the end of the video.

9. Do tutorials. Tutorials are especially popular on YouTube right now, with the search results for them spiking up every single year. People want to know

how to do things and gather new skills. This is a perfect way to show how your products work.

10. Compare two products. It doesn't necessarily have to be one of yours. Actually, don't do that because it can come off as a bit petty. It can be two more from your niche. Just take them and compare how the two of them work.

11. Perform a collaboration with a YouTuber. Reach out to a YouTuber in your niche and ask them if they want to make a video with you. Provided that you'll promote them on your channel, they just may say yes.

12. Talk about your business in depth. Include things like the history, where you got your idea for it, and more. You can really get into all the nitty and gritty of it.

You'll find that as time goes on, it will be easier to come up with YouTube content. However, let's be clear, you may have times where you hit a block, and the last thing you want to do is let yourself slip. This is why it's important to really keep yourself working on content all the time, and if you do find yourself running out of ideas, keep up with it. Keep this list on hand for inspiration.

Now, let's talk about growing, and how to really build your subscriber base and views by promotion.

The most important thing on YouTube isn't subscriber count. This may surprise some people, who put subscriber account above all else. Yes, subscriber count does count in some regards, but the real ticket to YouTube is the number of views you get. Good quality views count for everything on YouTube.

And to achieve these views, promotion is really key. This means doing things like researching keywords, promoting on other channels, and more. Let's look into them:

1. Cross-Promotion. This is something that needs to be talked about a bit; YouTube doesn't really work all on its own. It does much better when it's being promoted across another social media network, like Facebook, Instagram, or Twitter. You need to promote your videos on them by giving your viewers updates, showing behind the scene pictures, and more. This will help bring more viewers to your videos just as it will help bring more followers to your other accounts, which will guarantee more time to sell to them. Another thing to try is reaching out to other YouTubers and asking for shout outs or collaborations. "You scratch my back; I scratch yours" kind of deal.

2. Send out to all of your contacts. This includes email, phone numbers—

3. you name it. You need to promote your new content to everyone you know. Remember, your friends, family, and the people you know will want to support you, so you might get a subscriber just based on that. Not only that, but they may see a whole new side of you and your company that they generally wouldn't be able to enjoy.

4.   Use tags and keywords. Any keywords that you can't use in the title—use them in the description. Be sure to use tags as well, as they can make it easier for people to find you.

5.   Advertising. Of course, advertising is another option. But we'll discuss that at length next chapter.

6.   Include a call to action at the end of every single video. There's a reason why YouTubers always ask their followers to subscribe at the end of the video. And that's because it works. You can ask them to get notified as well by clicking the little bell beside the subscriber button. This actually works in getting people to subscribe and helps you rank better in the YouTube algorithm. There are of course people who will subscribe to you without any prompting just based on your content alone, but these are rare and far in between. Think of it this way: if every single other highly ranked YouTuber is doing it, why aren't you?

7.   Put a thumbnail into every single video. Thumbnails can make or break your channel, as it really defines as to whether or not someone will actually click on it. YouTube does give you the option of whether to add your own thumbnail or to pick one from three that are automatically given to you. Always pick to customize your own one. It looks far more professional.

8.   Stay on a schedule. Be consistent in when you post. If you post at 9 AM on a Friday, post every Friday at 9 AM. This will give people the sense that you're

taking this seriously and they'll learn to expect new content at the given time.

Now that we've gotten these tips out of the way, and you're fully prepared to start marketing and encourage viewership, now it's time to talk about your video setup. In this section, we're going to talk about what it takes to make quality videos, and how you should be preparing.

Setting Up Your Videos

People both overestimate and underestimate how much work goes into a YouTube channel. A well put-together YouTube channel can take hours of hard work, and there can be very little payoff for a while. You may not see results for months, or even years. How much money you choose to invest is ultimately up to you, but in this section, we're mostly just going to brush over exactly what you need equipment wise.

Equipment

In order to make good YouTube videos, the value of equipment we need is over-exaggerated. With everyone having a camera phone nowadays, anyone can make good quality videos with a selfie stick. While there are a lot of people with big YouTube channels who seemingly use the best equipment, the majority of people who use YouTube for marketing actually don't put thousands of dollars into it. In fact, just the opposite; most of them choose to invest in only the bare minimum of what they need. They understand that just because you have amazing equipment, there is no guarantee that your videos are going to be amazing.

This is even a philosophy carried out by actual professional filmmakers. The majority of content creators will tell you that sticking to simple ideas and simple ways of doing things will save your life when you're just starting out. You'll actually be thinking about making good content rather than trying to figure out and use the most expensive and advanced camera you could find. Good quality content is good quality content, no matter how it's made.

For choosing your equipment, I would say this: set your budget, don't go it, don't be impractical, and don't get suckered into buying something you're not actually going to use. Know what you need going in, and use this list to help you. The most basic YouTube kit tends to look something like this:

- Camera
- Tripod
- Video Editing Software
- Sound equipment
- Lighting

You may not need everything on this list. For example, if you're not shooting outside, you probably don't need sound equipment. If you're going to use natural lighting just at your window, why do you need lighting equipment? And let's not forget, if you don't know how to use Adobe Premiere Pro for video editing, don't get Adobe Premiere Pro. Stick to simple things, at least when you're still starting out and getting used to YouTube.

You can't make videos without a camera—to the surprise of nobody. You need something that will record high-quality video, at least 1080p. You really don't need a super expensive DSLR for this. You can get away with a high-quality camcorder (around $500 to $1,000) or a good webcam. If down the road you want to start making better content and really want to invest in your marketing, you can get a really good camera that's as fancy as you want.

These can be good or bad, depending on how much you want to spend, but you should be able to get a good one for under $100, but I would avoid a cheap one. Invest your money, because you need it to be stable and good quality. You don't want it to fall over and have your camera, whichever you're using, get damaged. Tripods can really change your game depending on what kind of content you want to make. There are a couple of different types of tripods, and what you need depends on your channel. But having one will really help upgrade your videos and make them look very professional. So it's worth it to invest your money.

Video Editing Software

We've already talked about video editing software, but I'm going to go more into a bit. Mostly because unlike with other social media networks, you really can't get around not using some kind of editing program on YouTube. There is a debate on whether or not you actually need to buy a program though. I really don't think you do.

There's no issue with actually getting something like Premiere Pro or Apple's Final Cut Pro if you're willing to take the time to learn how to use it. But there is a learning curve for both of them. What you need to remember is that there are plenty of programs out there which won't cost you hundreds of dollars a month. This is especially important if you don't want to include a lot of fancy editing in your videos. If you're just doing basic stuff, stick to the basic programs. If you want to learn something more complicated in the future, go for it, but until you're all in the habit of posting, then you can go for it.

Sound Equipment

One of the cardinal rules of good video content marketing is that you can get away with a bad picture, but you really can't get away with bad sound. If you have bad audio, it will ruin everything. It's just enjoyable to listen to. Cameras come with an internal mic, so you should be able to get away with that. However, if you're filming outside or if your videos heavily depend on sound, like dialogue, investing in sound equipment might not be a bad idea. This is especially important if you want ambient sound (room tone, or the sounds that you hear around you). The ones built into cameras just can't pick up on it. Mics can be as low as $150, but a good quality one will easily run you into the hundreds or even thousands.

Lighting

Lighting is also very underestimated. It can create mood, just making your audience feel things by just looking at the video. There are plenty of different lighting setups and ways of doing them out in the world. This means you really need to do your research, but you can pick up a relatively cheap set on Amazon. You might not even need lighting; again, if you can film just by a window in the daytime with the sun coming through, that's perfect. Natural lighting away works the best.

And that's pretty much it. These are the things you may need to run your YouTube channel. Again, you don't need all of these things, and you don't need to spend that much money. Try not to be allured by all the fancy terminology and equipment; you don't need it. You probably don't even know how to use it. Right now, you should just be focusing on putting out videos that work for your products and make them shine. You don't need to put thousands of dollars just in your equipment just for that to happen. Now, finally, our next section is for someone who may not be comfortable with the idea of being on camera. Yeah, we're going to talk about stage fright, just a tad.

Being On Camera

It's totally understandable. Being on camera is hard. This may be what holds you back from truly getting into YouTube marketing. Well, I have a secret for you: even the most experience videographer can get nervous when they're on camera. Hence, I've put together this list of things you can do to banish these jitters:

1. Make sure you're comfortable and well put together. This means wearing clothing that you look good in, but you'd also want your boss to see you in. Pick something clean, that fits well, and isn't covered in wrinkles or pet hair.

2. Take a lot of time to film. The first few times may be incredibly awkward, just speaking to the camera without anybody being there. It can feel a little strange at first. Hence, give yourself a lot of time so you won't feel rushed and will be able to give each of the takes a lot of time to get everything perfect.

3. Stay hydrated. Drink water or tea in between your takes. You don't want a raspy voice to ruin your video.

4. Place markers on the floor so that you know where to step if moving is necessary for the video. You will know exactly where to stop so that you're in the frame.

5. Rehearse until you can say what you have to say and you're completely comfortable. Don't just rattle off the script, though; this will make you sound uncomfortable and stiff, almost robotic. Remember, there is a person on the other side of that screen, and you really need to talk to them like you would in person. Speak naturally.

6. Take videos of yourself and watch for any nervous habits you have. This could be anything, from playing with your hair to chewing your lip or anything else you can think of. You can actively pull them under control once you know what they are.

7. Organization is really key here. Plan your scripts, your shooting schedule, your editing schedule, your posting schedule, everything. This will help you stay relaxed on camera if you're not constantly worrying about the fact that you're behind.

8. If you need a crew, pick people you trust. Some YouTube marketing doesn't require a crew—others definitely do. Or maybe you just don't want to do this alone. Regardless of your reason, make sure you choose people who you're comfortable doing things in front of and whom you trust to be sure that you look the best you possibly could. Bonus, if they're already experienced in making videos, they may already have their own equipment. They may show you how to use it.

9. Do whatever you need to help yourself relax. Anything you want, whether it's eating, exercise, singing really loudly, journaling, whatever it is. How relaxed you are will show, so it's best that you're in a good headspace. You could also try watching both bad YouTube videos and good YouTube videos to compare.

10. Laugh at yourself. If you do mess up, just laugh it off. It's probably funny, and it's no big deal. You'll

relax a lot easier if you don't take it so seriously. Remember, you can always start the take over again.

11. Limit your distractions. Turn off your phone. Tell your housemates/partner that you're filming and don't want to be disturbed. You won't be constantly distracted by everything around you. Just focus.

12. Forget about perfect. Perfection is not possible—at least when you first begin. Just be sure to do your best, and give yourself a lot of time to get things done. It will help keep you on track for the future. As long as you get the message out there and it looks good, it works. People don't want to see perfection in videos anyhow.

I hope this chapter on YouTube really helped bring forward points you may not have thought of so far. As you can see, YouTube is by far the most complicated of all the platforms, with a lot of hard work and energy going into it. It has to be, considering its content. However, I still say it's absolutely worth it.

Now, next chapter, we're going to talk about advertising on YouTube. Specifically, whether or not you should use them, how to get into them, and some more tips on how to advertise your content on the platform. Read on.

CHAPTER 7: YOUTUBE ADS

Hence, what is YouTube advertising? We've already talked about our content, what are we going to talk about now. YouTube advertising is basically the sole reason why YouTube can provide all of this crazy content for free. It's one of the world's biggest platforms for advertisers—and the numbers really don't lie.

The demand for YouTube advertising is truly insane. These stats are seriously crazy and show just how much YouTube advertising is totally worth it to invest in:

- YouTube mobile ads receive attention from viewers 8 out of 10 times. When you compare it to ads, which barely get our attention half the time, that's pretty crazy. Most people just choose to ignore ads, but for some reason, people don't ignore them on YouTube. For anyone looking into YouTube Ads, that should be very interesting.
- 95% of YouTube ads are audible. This is better than Facebook, where only 15% of their video ads are audible. By doing this, Google is able to track a sizeable lift in brand awareness, ad recall, and consideration.

These two stats may not seem like much, but they're really a game changer. Hence, in this chapter, I'm going to take you through all of the advertisement options that are offered on the platform and go through Google Ads. You'll have a thorough understanding of each of the 6 kinds of ads they offer, which will help you greatly planning your ad campaigns. Hence, let's get right into it.

YouTube Ad Formats

Now, on YouTube, there are six different kinds of ad formats. Three of them are video; TrueView ads, non-skippable video ads, and bumper ads. Then, there are the non-video ads; overlay ads, display ads, and cards and sponsored cards. Because YouTube is a video sharing platform, we're going to first talk about their video ad formats.

Because YouTube is a video-based platform, as we mentioned above, so it makes sense that videos are 100% one of the best ways to reach your audience and help build up your platform. We're going to go over each of the 3 formats quickly, and why they work.

TrueView Ads

These are quick skippable ads that appear on YouTube videos, at the very beginning. They're the perfect one for a beginner YouTube ad maker, and we're going to tell you why:

They're adaptable. You can pretty much show anything in a TrueView ad, from a tutorial, demonstrations of your products, a vlog, name it, you can put it there.

They're very low risk. These ads work, and they're very cost effective. Especially since you're only obligated to pay when they view has either been played all the way through (or for 3o seconds), and it's prompted an action (such as a click). Basically, you don't waste any money on them.

They reach a wide audience. Remember, YouTube is owned by Google. Hence, Google is able to take Google searches and use them to decide which ad to show who. This means you're able to take information from the two biggest search engines on the planet. This means they'll always reach the person who actually wants to see them.

True view ads are the first advertisement I would recommend that you do, but if it's not for you, we still have two more other video options to go.

Non-Skippable YouTube Ads

These are here to stay. They're also annoying. But people are learning to deal with them, mostly just ignoring them as they play in the background. They've become more tolerable since YouTube took the maximum length they could be from 30 seconds to 20 seconds long. There are two places a non-skippable ad can appear, at the beginning of your videos and the middle of your videos. Pre-roll ads can appear over a video of any length, while mid-roll ads only appear when a video is 10 minutes or longer.

This one is good if you want to go deeper into your story, and it requires a little build up. Adds that are skippable are skipped if they don't pull you in right away. However, if you can't skip at all, what's stopping someone from being intrigued? Your video does need to be hyper-focused, and you need to build up the tension.

You also need to be sure that the video really communicates to your audience exactly what you're trying to say, both audibly and visually. This way, when people do just look away to do something else, waiting for your video to just be over, they'll be listening anyway. You really need to think hard on this, as this is how you will truly succeed at non-skippable ads.

Not only are non-skippable ads great in that sense, but they also give you a lot of control over how much you spend. They're paid for on a cost-per-mile basis. This puts the reins right back in your hands. Plus, they're pretty effective for increasing brand awareness.

Finally, next we have:

Bumper Ads

This is the version of non-skippable ads that are slightly more tolerable. They last only six seconds at the most, and they appear at the end of YouTube videos. They're also paid for on a cost-per-mile basis. They're short, they're fast, and they are perfect if you plan on targeting mobile users. In fact, these are usually the ads you see when you watch YouTube on your phone.

There are great if you want to cut down the stigma against non-skippable ads. They're so short that most people won't bother actually leaving the screen, and really increase your exposure without actually driving anyone crazy.

And basically, that's what we've got for video ads. Now, let's talk about other forms of ads on YouTube, specifically non-video ad formats.

Non-Video YouTube Ad Formats

Maybe you're just not interested in making video ads, for whatever reason. Or, you want to make your video ads more interactive. Well, here's another way—non-video ad formats. Your options are overlay ads, sponsored cards, and display ads. Let's get into them.

Overlay Ads

Overlay ads are the advertisement banners who see along the bottom of a video. These vary depending on the ad but usually are just simple text ads or images on a banner.

Display Ads

These are the ads that appear above the video suggestion list. You've very likely seen them before—you may just not have noticed them. They're usually images.

Cards and Sponsored Cards

These are small popups that appear within the YouTube Player. These can be used to make your videos interactive. These are known to be effective, mostly because they're unobtrusive and people just don't notice them. They only expand when they've been clicked on. They do drive action, however, which makes them pretty effective. People like them because they're not being shoved in their faces.

Now, before you start with your ads, you're going to need a Google AdWords account. But first, I'm going to talk about how you make a great ad, and what each one needs.

Tips for a Great YouTube Ad

Now that you know all of the different ad formats, now you need to know how to use them well. These tips will take your ads from mediocre, to supercharged with information. These great practices and rules are to live by:

1. Treat your ads like you'd treat a YouTube video. You need to hook your viewers in your ad with engaging content that relevant to them. If you can show off what you do is a compelling way, this will impress your viewers, and will bring people to your channel and your services.

2. Keep titles simple. Ads play on YouTube just like regular videos do. They're searchable. So make sure people can find them. Your title needs to be relevant to what users search for, so people won't find it if it's not easy to find.

3. Use playlists. If you want to have more than one ad, you need to keep them all together. Someone may want to see them all. Or if you have videos relevant to it. This is a great way to get someone hooked into your channel, pulling them into your content and maybe towards buying something.

4. Make sure your channel has content first. Before you make any ads, be sure you have content. This is a mistake a lot of YouTuber marketers make, where they think that only the ads will help them and they don't need anything else. No, if somebody is interested in your ad, they want to know more. They want to know that you know what you're talking about. Be sure that there is a good collection of content on your channel.

5. Don't go too short. With an ad, you need to tell a story. A story that will capture people's notice and won't let them pull their eyes away from their screen. You can only do so much with a short ad, and while it can be tempting to fall into the idea of "the shorter, the better, so you don't lose people's attention," this doesn't always work. You just need to suck them into the story.

6. Use Call-To-Actions. TrueView ads let you add headlines and call-to-action buttons. These actually

work and make people stand up and pay attention. You've probably caught yourself doing it more than once. This makes ads more actionable, meaning people click on them.

7. Pay attention to what your competition is doing. Paying attention to your competition pays off in more ways than one, and if they're using ads, then check it out. You definitely shouldn't be copying them word for word, but it may bring you some inspiration and a couple of ideas.

Honestly, we could give you all the tips in the world, and the only thing that will really help you with making ads is the experience. Now, let's talk about AdSense and Google's Partnership Program—because it's worth it to consider.

Google AdSense and YouTube's
Partnership Program

I know what you're thinking: I want to get into YouTube to market my projects, not to make money. But why not do both? Why not get involved with AdSense and YouTube's partnership program if you can? If you've reached 1,000 subscribers and 4,000 viewing hours in less than 12 months, you can qualify for their program. That will bring you in money from ad revenue. The only thing you need to do is make sure that your content is 100% original and your own.

First, all you have to do is get an AdSense account. It's the program that is used by Google to pay out their YouTubers for making content. All you have to do is let them run ads on your videos, and you'll bring in money. Then, as long as you've got these 1,000 subscribers and 4,000 viewing hours in less than 12 months, plus no copyright claims, you can apply for their partnership program. You may not make a ton of money, but it will be something. There's no harm in trying, and why not get paid for advertising your business?

That's pretty much all I have to say about YouTube and advertising. Now, we're going to talk about Twitter, where social media marketing originated. Yes, you read that correctly.

CHAPTER 8: TWITTER 2020

Twitter is all about *now*. It's all about what's happening right now, right this second, as you read this. It moves fast and loves to move the conversation along with little push. Twitter is the place you go to have a conversation about anything from politics to cat videos. It's like the internet's very own news channel, with constant streams of information flocking in from every part of the globe.

Twitter loves this reputation of theirs and embraces it. It has a trending page specifically for this purpose so that people can find what people are talking about so they can join the conversation. Twitter wants people to continue using the platform to talk to people that they wish to talk to, about whatever they want to talk about.

In fact, it's thanks to that openness, of "talk to whomever you want," that we got social media marketing in the first place. When it was first created in 2006, their founders had no idea that they had just created a gold mine of opportunities. Thanks to the fact that Twitter users could actually simply send a message to their favorite celebrities or others with a tweet, they flocked to the platform. Eventually, celebrities got the memo and started to indulge them. Then, brands had the bright idea of "what if we had accounts on the platforms? Then we could talk to our customers directly." And so, social media marketing was born.

On Twitter, the beauty of the platform is that there are no limitations as who you can and can't talk to. Now, whether they answer you is a different scenario, but you still have the chance to speak with them directly. Thanks to this business model, there are thousands of businesses who use the platform to pull off a ton of their customer service requests that would've otherwise been dealt with over the phone. The days of waiting hours for a customer service agent was over; now all you had to do was send a tweet. And it worked.

To this day, Twitter is considered essential in many brand's business strategies, whether it's answering questions, retweeting happy customers, or even just chatting them up and listening to their opinion. Twitter is a goldmine for communicating with your customers, no matter what your business plan or type is. Check out this list of great stats on why Twitter is such a great platform, and why it works for so many happy businesses.

- 326 million people use Twitter every month, with 9% more people are using Twitter on a daily basis.
- 80% of the accounts on there are not from the USA. Twitter operates in 34 different languages, and it's available in 45 countries.
- 500 million tweets are sent out every single day. That's over 5,000 tweets every second (almost 6,000, actually; the number is 5,787). Keep in mind, that

number is pretty old (they released it in 2014 and haven't put out an updated one since). It's likely that the actual number is a lot bigger.

- Most of its future users will be adults over the age of 25. It's fairly popular with millennials, with 80% of its user base a part of the age group.
- 71% of users are finding news there. This only adds up to about 12% of Americans, but it's still a pretty large group. This is only encouraged by Twitter's insistence of being all about in-the-now. It's also likely what saved Twitter it's life.
- People are 31% more likely to remember what they saw on Twitter. This is opposed to just online web surfing. Who really knows why this is? Maybe we just love Twitter. This is an interesting stat, and if you could somehow find a way to make it work in your strategy, go for it.
- 85% of social media business Twitter users say that having a Twitter account for business is important.
- 40% of users have said they have made a purchase based on a tweet.

Hence, what are you waiting for, really? Twitter is the perfect place to take part in customer service, and not only that, but it's a great place to make connections with other people who may not have otherwise heard of you.

But let's be real: Twitter can be grueling work. You have to tweet upwards of 10 times a day. There isn't really a magic number of how much you have to tweet in one day to really get noticed, but the general consensus is that you have to keep up with what's going on. Meaning, you have to continually tweet again and again so that you stay at the top of the feed. It thrives on fast moments and constant engagement.

Twitter moves incredibly fast, so it's not hard to get lost in the shuffle of it all.

Hence, the big question is, why should you be on Twitter?

Maybe the facts up above haven't convinced you? Or maybe because you're just not sure it's a good fit? Maybe you've heard bad things about it and the people on the platform? Or maybe you've heard that it's gotten out of style and that the only people on it are freaks and geeks?

Twitter is still a great place to go to for social media marketing. It's full of amazing people that you can talk to. You can communicate with customers across the globe. You can use it to discover leads and people to collaborate with. You're constantly staying in the now, and able to reply to things in real time. You'll always know what's going on, anywhere in the world.

Now, let's get into Twitter, shall we?

Creating your Twitter

I would say, one of the best things about Twitter is the fact that it hasn't changed all that much. The platform still looks generally the same way it did years ago, and its basic concept hasn't really changed all that much. Building a great profile has pretty much stayed the same as well, which is nice, really.

A complete Twitter profile does more than just slap a pretty face onto your brand. It helps build trust with your audience, help you appear in search results easier, and helps give your customers the full idea of what exactly you're about. You want your customers to immediately have an idea of who you are when they head to your profile. Hence, here's how to do it right:

Pick a great picture for your cover and your profile image: Don't make these the same. Your cover photo should absolutely be different from your cover image. If you want to use your logo for your profile picture, that is absolutely an option. It's simple and requires little effort on your part.

Write a great bio: You have fewer characters in your bio than you get in your tweets, only 160. You can still get the most out of it though, and you'd be amazed at just how much you can say in just 160 characters. You can follow these tips to write an amazing Twitter bio for your brand:

Take inspiration from other people in your niche. If you're really finding yourself stalling on what you want to write, there's no harm in checking out other people's profiles for inspiration, especially other brands. They likely have already been in the game for months or even years, and know exactly how to draw their audience in for wanting more.

Introduce yourself. Really, the first tip to writing any bio is to just focus on who you are and what you need the audience to know about yourself. Add important qualities about your brand, share what you do, and be sure to let people know what they should be expecting from you.

Stick to the essentials. You only have 160 characters, so you need to use them well. This means summing up what you do in as little characters as possible, without overdoing it. If there is a phrase or a word or a syllable that is not necessary, delete it. You're just wasting space. However, be sure to use all of the characters that you have. A recent study has claimed that more characters in your bio mean more followers.

Show your personality. Your bio is almost like a trailer to what your tweets are going to be like. You need to show off what people will expect from you, whether it's jokes, news updates, or anything else. Just give them a taste.

Use keywords. Unlike Instagram bios, Twitter bios are very, very searchable—which means that people can Google what's in your bio, and you will show up. Hence, be sure to use a lot of keywords and phrases to do with your brand.

Mention any awards or any other recognition you've gotten. This is important to show, as it proves outright that you know your stuff. Just don't overdo it, and be humble.

Use emojis. Emojis are great at conveying brands in things like personality, and they can convey as much in one character as 5 to 10 words can. They also add a bit of excitement to your bio.

Put in your brand hashtag, and that's it. Hashtags may be born on Twitter, but they're a bit of a hit or miss, especially in bios. There have been studies that point to the fact that accounts with fewer hashtags in their bios actually have more followers. It can look spammy. This means you should be sticking to your brand or company hashtag if you have one. If you don't, avoid them altogether.

Finally, if you have an Instagram account, there's no reason why you can't just copy and paste your bio from there to Twitter (or vice versa, but Instagram's bios are slightly shorter). You may have to edit them slightly, but it could work if you're keeping it really simple.

Once your bio is done, you're going to have to complete and optimize your profile.

What does this mean?

An optimized Twitter profile is about more than just sharing your name and handle. It's about boosting the visual impact of your profile. It can help people find you easier. This means doing the following:

- Adding your location
- Adding your website
- Add other links to social media

If you can, you should also get verified. Getting verified is tricky on Twitter, as there are really no guidelines on how to actually get verified. The biggest thing that will help you get verified is public interest. If it's shown that people are really interested in what you have to say, this will fast track you on the lane of getting that valuable blue checkmark beside your name. And it is valuable; 85% of consumers are more likely to buy from brands they trust. There is a level of trust afforded to these accounts who do have that little blue checkmark that is not extended to the ones without.

That's pretty much all we have to say about building your profile. Now, we're going to talk about how you can use Twitter to get optimal results. It's one of the best platforms to give your followers update, and you need to know how to use it to really help push your narrative.

Learning to Listen

If you really want to help keep your viewers informed and that's it, you're really not taking advantage of one of the things that make Twitter so great. And how can you take advantage of everything that makes Twitter great? You can learn to listen.

Brands that pursue actual, active listening feel the benefits significantly. They learn more about competitors, instantly and learn about how people see your brand. You're able to get real-time information of what people are thinking now, no polls necessary (you can run polls on Twitter, to be clear).

Not only that but you need to pay attention to what's happening online. Twitter is the perfect place to do this. You can check out trending pages, and do research on what's going in the world. You can look to see what people are talking about, who they're talking to, who they're following, who they agree with, and so much more. You can do research on buzzwords and your competitors and SEO. This is all useful information, and you can find it on Twitter by not just using it to talk to your customers.

Another reason why you should be listening? You can find influencers and other members in your field who you can learn from. Paying attention to what's going on surrounding a certain topic is a sure sign of a pro, and it helps really establish how your followers see you. Especially if you regularly refer to it with your tweets.

And finally, it's time to start tweeting.

Tweeting Effectively

Being effective on Twitter can be the most grueling part of the process. Unlike other social media networks, where you only need to make a post maybe 1 to 3 times per day, sometimes even less than that. Twitter is different in that you need to post consistently throughout the day, sometimes up to 10 times every day. And because Twitter is done where it's in the now, and there's a constant stream of new tweets coming in every day, it can be easy just to get shuffled down into the abyss of the internet in less than 30 minutes.

This means that you need to post at least 5 times a day and while they definitely don't need to be fancy. You don't need to use every 280 characters. But what you do have to do is make sure that each one is quality, and emulates what you want people to see when they think of your brand. Here are some basics to writing a great tweet:

1. Help your audience. You need to create content that your audience will see, and they will use. It needs to be useful in some way, whether it's fulfilling a need or entertaining them. Every tweet should be sent out to accomplish this.

2. Keep as short as possible. Just as we mentioned above, you don't need to use all the characters every single time you tweet. All you really have to do is accomplish what you set out to do with your tweet.

3. Use hashtags, but don't overdo them. Hashtags will help more people see the tweets, meaning that more people will find you and follow you if they like what they see. But overloading your tweets with hashtags come off as incredibly spammy and weird looking. Stick only using one or two per tweet, and make sure they make sense in regards to the actual tweet.

4. Mix up your content to help drive engagement. Engagement, such as retweets, will help get you seen more by people who haven't seen you. Use video, images, links, and gifs. Video content gets a lot of engagement on Twitter, with users reporting that the vast majority of them, 82%, watch and enjoy video content. They want to see more of this, so why not give it to them? Gifs are another way to make fun tweets and are an easy way to insert a bit of personality into them. If animated or live action fun little pictures fit your brand, go for them.

5. Post frequently, and at the right time. You only have about 25 minutes before a tweet gets about all the engagement it's going to get. It means you need to tweet regularly to attract and engage followers, post between 12 pm and 6 pm, and scheduling your tweets. Scheduling your tweets gives you the advantage of not having to worry about forgetting or not.

6. Talk to your audience. This is one of the most important things you can do on any social media network, but especially on Twitter. This is because Twitter has given the impression that it is very personal. You can literally throw your question directly at the company. But communicating effectively with your followers requires a lot more than just replying to their comments. There's a whole lot of other things you can do to really pump up the effectiveness of your campaign:

    *   Follow your network. This means following your followers. You can learn about them, such as their interests, needs, wants, preferences, and much more. This can help you come up with future services.
    *   Respond ASAP. The quicker you respond, the better it is for you. People expect an instant response when they go straight to the business themselves. This means as soon as you see something, reply to it.

- Retweet and like their tweets. If there are good reviews of your products or your brand, why aren't you replying to them in some way or another? This will help your followers feel good.
- Get interactive. Ask your followers questions, run polls for feedback or their opinion, and tag them in posts. An @ mention is an easy way to drive some attention their way, and they'll likely return the favor.
- Occasionally giving your followers a bit of attention will really help lift their spirits and help keep them happy. It tells them that you actually care what they think and about making them happy. Providing good customer service is why you're on Twitter in the first place, so you should absolutely be using all of these options to the best as possible.
- Be personal when you do answer to them. Don't just copy and paste your answer. Too many brands do this, especially when they're dealing with a crisis. Be actual personal to each and every person who gets in touch with you.

7. Use humor and personality in your tweets. Don't be afraid to get a little more casual with Twitter. Twitter is designed around having a conversation, so you should be answering as you would be in real life. Being lighthearted and not so stiff and impersonal will help you gain customers and engage with your followers the way you would a friend. You'll seem

more reachable to them. Do this by including things like emojis and answering in the way that you'd picture the brand answering if it was a person.

There are a lot of our tips on writing and creating tweets. Now we're going to talk about some tips on how to grow, and also to make things slightly easier on yourself.

Twitter Growth

Growing on Twitter is a tough gig. It can take a lot of hard work, with very little reward. Obviously, the easiest way to grow is to make sure that you're putting quality content out there and doing so regularly. However, what if you could make it easier? This section is all about making things slightly easier for you, but at the same time growing in an organic way.

1. Reuse content. Twitter has a retweet feature for a reason, guys. Use it. You can retweet your old tweets, mostly information that's still relevant like reminders that there's an event coming up. You could also tweet old articles with updates, or compare then and now.
2. Follow and talk about what you know. The easiest way to really grow is to talk about what you know and who you are as a brand. If you just continually put out content relating to that, people will know what to expect from you, and you'll automatically grow. You should also be following big brands that

have to do with your niche to help yourself make these connections.

3. Talk with other brands. Don't just follow them, actually engage with a conversation with them. Reply to their tweets. Challenge them. Support them. Maybe even tease them a bit; people love to see brands teasing each other on Twitter. Just google "Denny's Roasting Other Brands," and you'll see what I mean.

4. Use ads. Finally, we're talking about ads. That's what our next section is about, where you'll learn how to do ads and whether or not you should use Twitter ads.

Twitter Ads

Getting a bit of a boost, the right way, not bots, isn't a bad idea when it comes to Twitter. Or any social media network, for a matter of fact. Some people feel like it's cheating if they advertise on social media to get more followers and likes, but I disagree. After all, big brands do advertising all the time. They advertise their products, why shouldn't you? It's difficult to do this all by yourself, and as we've talked about before, it's not hard for your tweets to just get lost in the Twitter abyss.

Before you get started with Twitter advertising, you need to make a Twitter Ad account. This is where Twitter monitors and keeps tracks of the advertising services you use. The webpage is ads.twitter.com. All you have to do is enter where you are from and what your timezone is. It's very simple. Similar to Facebook ads, Twitter walks you through the entire process, no issues whatsoever. However, one downside to Twitter ads is that they don't have nearly the variety that Facebook or YouTube ads have. Actually, they're limited only down to three. This may not seem like a lot, but really, these options are all you really need on Twitter. Plus, each of these options is flexible in their own way.

Promoted Tweet: this is when you take a tweet of your choice, preferably one that has already done well. Twitter Ads then takes the tweet and have it appear on people's feeds. Specifically, people who don't follow you but still fall within your demographic and who will be interested in what you have to say. It appears and feels exactly like a normal tweet would, the only ad on is that it has the word "sponsored" on it.

Promoted Account: this works exactly the same as a sponsored tweet, but it's your whole account this time. If you've been on Twitter long enough, you'll notice these sidebars that Twitter show you of people who you might be interested in but don't follow. Hence, Twitter takes your account and puts you in that sidebar, and you're labeled with the word "sponsored" so they know you're an ad. This works pretty well if you're looking to engage followers.

Promoted Trend: this is the one that isn't available to most people. It's only available to large companies who can get meetings with representatives of Twitter. It's an entire process even to see if you're eligible for it. However, it's still worth checking out if you are curious. This is where Twitter takes a hashtag or subject of your choice and puts it on their trending page, basically making the whole world look at it. This works especially well if you want to have a lot of exposure on one product all at the same time, as it brings with it a lot of tweets. People tweet about what's on the trending page, remember?

Twitter may not be as popular as it used to be, but it's showing no sign of going away anytime soon. Its users are dedicated to it, and log on constantly. They're making money for the first time ever from ad revenue. It's a great place to connect with customers and people who are also in your niche— if you're someone who wants to take part in the conversation and want to put themselves as a true expert in whatever subject they are.

Twitter may be hard work, but connecting and bonding with your customers on the platform is truly worth it. The fact that you can communicate with them one-on-one is brilliant and works well—plus, we do have to pay homage to the fact that without Twitter, there would be no social media marketing. We really can't forget that.

And finally, we've almost reached the end of this book—but I still have a bit more for you. Our conclusion is next.

CONCLUSION

Thank you for making it through to the end of *Social Media Marketing 2020*. Let's hope it was informative and able to provide you with all of the tools you need to achieve your goals—whatever they may be.

The next step is to go out there and get started with your social media marketing. Just get out there and start doing it. Taking the first step towards your goal will help you drastically in just getting things over with. Taking that first step may seem very difficult, but it's really all about taking that first step.

Remember—all the information in this book was truly written to help you, not bombard you until you're overwhelmed and confused. I truly hope that this has helped you and that you're not so confused anymore. The world of social media marketing is a bit vicious.

Just remember, keep grinding. Don't give up. Giving up will only lead to failure, and a year from now, you'll be kicking yourself for not grinding along the first time. Consistency and quality—that's where your strengths lie in social media.

No matter what platform you end up choosing, remember that it's likely always going to be changing. Not only that, but there is a new social media network every day now, so there's probably going to be another big one before the year is over. The world is constantly changing, so you have to keep up.

Hence, pay attention. Pay close attention to what's happening in the world now with social media. It's never going to stop changing and evolving, so you need to pay attention. New features will be added; there will be new ways of doing things, new equipment, new ad formats—you name it. Just understand that there will always be something new to learn about the subject, no matter how much you read or do.

Hence, get out there, and start social media marketing like the pro you are now.

Finally, if you found this book useful in any way, a review on Amazon is always appreciated!